The Sport
of
Olympic-Style
Weightlifting

Training for the Connoisseur

Praise for Carl Miller

"After reading Carl's *The Sport of Olympic-Style Weightlifting: Training for the Connoisseur*, I'm amazed at his insight and ease of expressing to all the "secret and analyzing process" that all serious weightlifters would give their eyeteeth to learn. This is the most comprehensive treatise that any weightlifter could hope for. During my years of training, I would have welcomed such great information. When reading this book, pay special attention to the detail that Carl expresses to each of you, because of the different structure we each have. He gives me the desire to start lifting again. Anyway, this is a must have detailed book for all serious weightlifters."

—Frank Spellman, former US National and Olympic Weightlifting Champion

"I met Carl Miller in 1975 as an aspiring Class 1 Lifter. Five years later, I qualified for the Olympic Team at 90 kg. I can honestly say without Carl's expertise, guidance and encouragement, this would never have happened. This book is a compilation of proven training techniques that can help any lifter, no matter what level, to stay strong, flexible and functional into their 80s and beyond. As a successful Physical Therapist of 34 years, I've learned from Carl, and I pass this on to my patients to stay strong and enjoy Life!"

—Luke Klaja, Physical Therapist,
1980 US Olympic Weightlifting Team, Master's National Record

"Virtually all physicians consider regular exercise to be a crucial component of good health. Carl Miller has drawn on his background in physiology and his lifetime of experience in developing these exercise programs that are good from beginners to international competitors. The book he has written is extremely well thought out, thorough, detailed, and sensible. I highly recommend Carl's book and program to all people interested in this style of exercise."

—Robert M. Bernstein, MD, FACE

arl Miller's book, *The Sport of Olympic-Style Weightlifting: Training for the Connoisseur*, is a very unique book in its ability to combine all the necessary elements required to become a champion weightlifter with the training methodology and programs to achieve success. I especially enjoyed reading and studying the Intensity programs from countries like Russia, Bulgaria, Cuba, and so forth in Chapter 8 and how to determine and use the "K Value" in Chapter 9.

"Many weightlifters never understand or discover the tricks to proper peaking, which Carl explains with ease in Chapter 10, and how to "Cluster Train" in preparation for competition, in Chapter 11. This book is a wealth of information not only for the novice weightlifter, but for the experienced, competition tested weightlifter as well.

"I thoroughly enjoyed the Introduction on Carl Miller's education and experience. It sheds light on how Carl trained to compete and how he trained his athletes to compete and why both he and his athletes were and are so successful. It is always fun and educational to read about and learn from athletes of the past. With the scientific advances since those times, there is no reason that we shouldn't be #1 in the World in Olympic weightlifting and this book may be the catalyst to effect that change. Great job Carl—two thumbs up!"

—Doug Briggs, PhD, CSCS. Director of Human Performance-US Army/MWR, two-time Masters Pan-American Champion and two-time Masters National Champion—USAW. Author of *Built for Strength: A Basic Approach to Weight Training Success for Men and Women*

The Sport
of
Olympic-Style
Weightlifting

Training for the Connoisseur

Carl Miller

with
Kim Alderwick

SUNSTONE
PRESS

Santa Fe

Sunstone books may be purchased for educational, business, or sales promotional use.
For information please write: Special Markets Department, Sunstone Press,
P.O. Box 2321, Santa Fe, New Mexico 87504-2321.

Book and Cover design ► Vicki Ahl
Body typeface ► Myraid Pro
Printed on acid free paper

Library of Congress Cataloging-in-Publication Data

Miller, Carl, 1940-
    The sport of Olympic-style weightlifting : training for the connoisseur / by Carl Miller
with Kim Alderwick
        p. cm.
    ISBN 978-0-86534-811-0 (softcover : alk. paper)
    1. Weight lifting. I. Alderwick, Kim. II. Title.
GV546.3.M55 2011
796.41--dc22
                            2011008346

WWW.SUNSTONEPRESS.COM
SUNSTONE PRESS / POST OFFICE BOX 2321 / SANTA FE, NM 87504-2321 /USA
(505) 988-4418 / ORDERS ONLY (800) 243-5644 / FAX (505) 988-1025

The Sport
of
Olympic-Style
Weightlifting

Training for the Connoisseur

Carl Miller
with Kim Alderwick

Contents

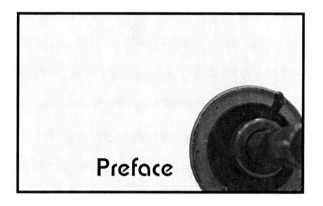

Preface

Many lifters do not achieve their goals because to get to the top, you have to be a real connoisseur.

Many lifters do not know what they want to do.

If they know what to do, they do not know how to do it.

If they know how to do it, they do not want to work hard enough to achieve it.

If they work hard enough, they do not know how to eliminate the errors and omissions.

Do not be afraid of getting to the top because once you get there, you have less competition. Everybody else has eliminated themselves. They have found their niche.

—Carl Miller

Acknowledgments

To Kim Alderwick who did the vast majority of editing to the manuscript.
To Jan Orcutt who greatly helped in the final editing.
To Shane Miller for content advice.
And to all the fine coaches and athletes I came in contact with.

Introduction
by
Kim Alderwick

Olympic lifting may be one of the purest of all sports. It distills the quickness, agility, power and coordination essential to all athletic endeavors into a single, brief motion. It truly is a sport for connoisseurs. There's nothing like it.

True story. I was interviewing Carl Miller in the main office of his gym when a man came to the door. "Carl Miller? I just moved back to town, and saw you still had a gym here. I want to thank you. I was in your gym class at Carlos Gilbert Elementary, 30 years ago, and you changed my life." The universe sure has a way of punctuating a moment.

Carl and I had been talking about his life and work, and this interruption was perfectly timed. In a few words, this man summed up why Miller and I had been talking at all. His contributions to the field of Olympic weightlifting have been enormous, and his influence within the field of fitness has been equally so.

Miller was first introduced to weightlifting by his stepfather, Leonard McRae. McRae almost lost his leg in World War II and was told to exercise to maintain the function of his knee. He worked out regularly and sometimes he brought his 12-year-old stepson with him. One day, McRae took the boy to a gym in Hollywood. Not just any gym, it was Bert Goodrich's chrome-and-leatherette-appointed "Gym to the Stars."

Goodrich was the first Mr. America, earning the title in 1938, and his gym was training central for Hollywood luminaries like Jayne Mansfield, Marilyn Monroe, Fess Parker and Mario Lanza. But Bert didn't just cater to actors. Serious, competitive athletes trained there, too. UCLA and USC track and field athletes worked out at Bert's, as well as a number of Olympic medalists and contenders. Mel Whitfield, 400-m Olympic gold medal winner was a regular Bert's guy, along with Parry O'Brien, a two-time Olympic gold medalist in the shot put and Olympic Hall of Famer. On occasion, John Davis, a twelve-time Olympic-style weightlifting national champion and two-time Olympic gold medal winner, trained there, too. Frank Spellman, a 1948 Olympic weightlifting champion, was a regular.

Then there were the body builders, like the legendary Roy Hilligenn. Hilligenn won both the Mr. America and Mr. Universe titles, before the wide use of steroids. Miller remembers that Hilligenn was exceptional in that he trained for body building three days a week and Olympic lifting three days a week.

Miller trained regularly with his stepfather, and about once a month, they would drive down to Venice Beach. This was California in the fifties, blue skies, clear water and a nation breaking into an age of post-war prosperity and promise. Everything, and anything, was possible. Men and women began to explore the limits of weight training and body building, combining it with other disciplines. While some lifted weights, their skin oiled and glistening in the sun, hand balancing, acrobatics and gymnastics were part of the show, too. A new age was dawning, and a new consciousness of fitness and health were a part of it. So was Miller.

He was 14 when McRae introduced him to Frank Spellman, the middle-weight lifting champion of the 1948 Olympics. Carl was awed by Spellman, and after a time, he mustered the courage to ask Spellman to teach him the lifts. Spellman looked him over. "Let me see ya' do a high pull. Do a squat." Carl did both and Spellman agreed, "Yeah, you can train with me."

Of all the people Miller met at Bert's, Spellman would be the most influential. Spellman had moved to California from York, Pennsylvania, where he was a machinist at York Barbell and trained with the legendary Bob Hoffman, considered the Father of American Weightlifting. The factory had a gym where workers were encouraged to train and numerous important lifters emerged from it. When Spellman moved West, he brought his love for lifting with him. It was Spellman who taught Miller the Olympic lifts, and they trained at the gym regularly.

After a time, like many lifters today, Spellman set up his own garage gym and invited his friends to come by. Olympic shot put medalist, Dave Davis, trained in the garage, and so did Dallas Long, another Olympic shot putter and gold medal winner. Discus champion Jay Silvester was another. Dave Sheppard, yet another Olympic medalist, came by from time to time. Paul Anderson would show up, too. Miller remembers Anderson picking up a 200-pound dumbbell with his fingers, calling to Spellman, "Hey Spellman, I bet you can't do this!" Years later, Miller would hear a Russian lifter refer to Anderson as "the Eighth Wonder of the World."

Spellman's low garage ceiling spawned a theory in weightlifting that one hears to this day, at least in Miller's gym and always in jest. Miller was too tall to jerk the bar into a full extension so Spellman would assure him, "If you can clean it, you can jerk it." It wasn't just Miller's height and Spellman's low ceiling that lent this statement its truth. There was another reason. At the time, weightlifting rules prohibited contact between the bar and the lifter's leg. This forced the lifter to hold the bar slightly out front throughout the lift. When this rule was eliminated, lifters were able to move more weight.

(Over the years, many rules of weightlifting have changed, including the weight classes and the use of kilos instead of pounds. At one time, too, Olympic medals were granted for both lifts *and* a meet total. This will explain to the reader changing references to pounds and kilos, and an occasional mention of an obsolete weight class.)

Miller worked with Spellman for several years, and Spellman coached him to the Teenage National Weightlifting Championships. At age 19, weighing 198 pounds, Miller snatched 245 pounds, earned the first place trophy for his division, and set a new national record.

College followed. Miller attended UC Berkeley, where he earned a Bachelor of Science in Education, with an emphasis in exercise physiology and biomechanics. He earned his Masters at the University of Arizona. He organized Olympic weightlifting teams at both schools before an unusual stint in the Peace Corps opened the door for international travel.

President John F. Kennedy established the Peace Corps in 1961. It was a popular program offering young Americans the opportunity to provide service overseas. One Peace Corps initiative promoted competitive athletics as a means of building national pride among developing countries, and the Corps actively recruited coaches for the program. Miller applied and was among the second group of this kind, arriving in Colombia in 1963. He succeeded Jim Curry, a former basketball player with the St. Louis Hawks.

Miller lived in Cali, the sport capital of Colombia, where he assisted Olympic weightlifting coach, Ney Lopez, and worked with the track and field team, helping with strength training. He enjoyed some noteworthy success while he was there. One of his track athletes was runner, Pedro Grajales. Miller helped him shave an incredible 3/10 of a second from his time in the 200 m, in just three months. This was a great achievement, particularly because Grajales was already 29. With the new time, he qualified for the 1964 Tokyo Olympics. Another of Miller's athletes, Alvaro Mejia, ran second in the marathon at the Pan Am Games. In addition to his coaching assignments, Miller taught anatomy at the University of Cali.

The Colombian sport program was already underway when Miller arrived. Coaches from the Soviet Union, East Germany, Czechoslovakia, Romania and Japan were invited to Colombia to conduct weightlifting clinics, and Miller became acquainted with a number of them. It was an opportunity to learn the training methods employed behind the "Iron Curtain," a part of world from which little information was available. Miller traveled throughout South America with the Colombian team, visiting every country except Venezuela.

At the end of his Peace Corps assignment, Miller was invited to weight train the women's volleyball team affiliated with the Nichibo Textile Factory, in Kobe, Japan. To augment the small salary they offered, he also worked as athletic director for the Canadian Academy and conducted research in exercise physiology at Miyagi University. And in the nascent days of Japanese baseball, Miller even weight trained the Hankyu Braves, and he worked with the Japanese weightlifting team.

The volleyball players were recruited from the southern island, where the population tended to be taller. They worked in the factory during the day and after eight hour work shifts, trained for seven hours at night. Miller is still astonished by the intensity of their work ethic and clearly recalls an especially grueling practice drill. The drill involved diving onto the floor into a shoulder roll, then springing quickly to the feet to hit a ball back over the net. The balls were moving fast and were fired off continuously, forcing the woman to immediately jump to her feet and dive again. The drill lasted fifteen minutes, after which the women literally crawled from the court, the floor slick with sweat.

Miller marveled at the effort the women dedicated to their sport and when he asked how they could work so hard, night after night, they told him, "We do it for our country." They were rewarded for their hard work when the team was selected to represent Japan at the 1968 Summer Olympics in Mexico City, and Miller was there when the women of the Nichibo volleyball team won the gold medal. They returned to Japan as heroes.

After three years of coaching in Japan, Miller returned to the US, and as the saying goes, when one door closes another opens. Though Olympic lifting had long been popular in Europe and South America, it was largely unknown to American athletes and sports enthusiasts. It was Olympic weightlifting's relative obscurity that provided Miller with the opportunity of a lifetime.

The Olympics had gone poorly for the Americans in 1972. To address the problem, the Olympic organizing committee explored the possibility of a national coach and wanted to test the strategy with a lesser-known sport. Prior to this, there had been no national coaches for the American Olympic teams. They chose Olympic lifting because of its relative obscurity and contacted Miller. When he told them his terms, that he needed to travel to find talent and to study training methods used outside the US, they turned him down. A year later, the committee returned to offer him the position and agreed to his terms. He took the job and traveled extensively for the next five years, 1973–1978.

During the week, Miller taught physical education in the basement gym of Carlos Gilbert Elementary School in Santa Fe, New Mexico and on weekends, traveled around the country, scouting gyms and athletes. There were a number of communities where Olympic lifting seemed to thrive. Not surprisingly, York, Pennsylvania, where York Barbell was headquartered, was an important bastion of the sport. And there were other towns across the country where Olympic lifting was practiced, small towns like Safford, Arizona; Willimantic, Connecticut; Daytona Beach, Florida; Marietta, Georgia; Ames, Iowa; and visited the famous Central Falls Weightlifting Club in Rhode Island, under the coaching of Joe Mills.

During this time, Miller traveled to many large, international competitions and clinics throughout Eastern Europe and Germany. He toured training halls in Bulgaria, Germany, Poland, Romania, Japan and Russia and met with coaches and athletes. Sometimes it was after a meal, sharing "national beverages," that he learned the most. He studied, took notes and returned from each trip with more information and more insight about his sport. He learned directly from the athletes and coaches who dominated it.

Earlier in his career, Miller learned that Japanese athletes trained for Japan. During trips to the eastern bloc countries, he met athletes who trained for their lives. In poor nations where opportunities were so few, athletics opened doors to better food, apartments and a standard of living otherwise beyond the reach of most people. Needless to say, the athletes trained very, very hard. In Bulgaria, they trained six hours a day, every day. When Miller asked how the body could tolerate that level of stress and exertion, the response was cool, "There are casualties in every war." Competition was taken very seriously.

While attending an international coaches clinic in Sofia, Bulgaria, Miller had the opportunity to spend time with Ivan Abadjiev, the great Bulgarian lifter and coach. Over the course of five days, the two spoke at length about lifting and training. Abadjiev acknowledged the importance of science in the development of training programs but warned of its limitations; "Observe nature," was his advice. "Watch animals, how they move, accelerate, recruit power. There is information there, too."

The Bulgarians maintained a dogmatic program in which one either succeeded or failed. The Russians were more adaptable to the specific needs of certain individuals. One world champion, Kurentsov, was permitted to train just five or six hours a week. The Hungarians and East Germans were somewhat flexible, as well, permitting small deviations from target goals.

In 1974, Miller toured Germany, France, Spain and England with a group of lifters, aged twenty-three and under. The group was scheduled to compete in four meets in sixteen days, and the lifters set new personal bests at each one. It was an epic accomplishment that won praise from European coaches and lifters, alike.

It was not all hard work and weightlifting on these trips. Miller enjoyed touring the sights and the opportunity to experience the unique cultures of the places he visited. There were misadventures, as well. In Moscow, for the World Championships in 1975, Miller decided a jog through Red Square might help shake off a little jet lag. He was arrested on sight. Jogging through Red Square was forbidden. For this gesture of "disrespect," Miller spent a few hours in a Moscow jail cell, just long enough for the US ambassador to apologize to authorities.

He traveled with his American lifting team to the 1976 Montreal Olympics. Phil Grippaldi finished third in the clean and jerk. Bruce Wilhelm was second in the snatch and placed fifth in his division. When Lee James earned a silver medal, it was the American lifting team's last shining moment at a fully attended Olympic Games. In 1984, the year of the Eastern bloc and the Soviet Union's boycott of the Olympics, two American lifters won medals. It was not until 2000, when Tara Nott won a gold medal, and Cheryl Haworth won the bronze, that the US again medaled at an openly attended Olympic Games.

After almost five years as the first U. S. Olympic Coaching Coordinator in any sport, Miller resigned. The Olympic committee's new administration preferred a different model of promoting lifting in the US They invited lifting greats from overseas to perform demonstrations for the American audience, with the idea that this would stimulate interest in Olympic lifting. It was a top-down system, at odds with Miller's bottom-up, cultivate talent and build a team, approach. Travel was curtailed and recruiting came to an end. It was time for something new.

Between 1977 and 1982, Miller held summer weight training camps in and around Santa Fe. Many important contributors to the sport attended. Kim Goss, now editor of the excellent strength sport magazine, *Bigger, Faster, Stronger*, was a student. Halsey Miller and Derrick Crass attended, and so did Marty Cypher, later a coaching inductee to the Olympic Weightlifting Hall of Fame. Olympic competitors, Luke Klaja, weightlifting, and Sam Walker, shot put, also attended. Cory and Jeff Everson were also in Santa Fe for Miller's course. Cory is a six-time Ms Olympia and Jeff, former editor of *Muscle and Fitness Magazine*, also claimed a Mr. USA body building title. Dr. John Garhammer, the respected sport scientist, was one of Miller's campers, too. A close associate and coach for chess champion Bobby Fischer, John Kay, came, too.

Miller's credentials also include consulting with strength coaches for the Dallas Cowboys, San Francisco 49ers, New England Patriots and Chicago Bulls. And since 1982, he has owned and run a gym in Santa Fe, New Mexico. Carl and Sandra's Conditioning Center serves clients from 9 to 90 years of age, addressing general fitness, cross-training and rehabilitation needs. Memberships of 10 years duration, or longer, are not unusual there. And quite literally, gym members at both ends of this age spectrum have participated in Miller's non-sanctioned "fun" meets, competing in the Olympic lifts and enjoying the challenge.

Miller has published five books on the subject of weightlifting and fitness. His early books were the sole primers for lifting in the US, based on methods and training tools of the Eastern Europeans, who dominated the sport. They are still read today.

As for his own weightlifting achievements, Miller's best lift in the Snatch, before retiring at age 23, was 255 pounds, and 320 in the Clean and Jerk. Years later, at age 51, he lifted in the 198 pound class and Snatched 270 and Clean and Jerked 341. Carl Cleaned and Jerked 352 in practice a couple of years later.

Miller's work is based on years of observation and sound principles of exercise physiology. The Europeans conducted the research, published the papers and tested the limits of their athletes. Miller takes their science, his experience, and applies them.

Notes

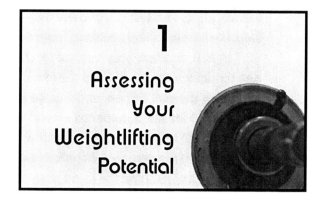

1
Assessing Your Weightlifting Potential

During my travels in the 1960s, 70s and 80s, I was privileged to study with some of the best coaches in the history of the sport. I learned a great deal from them, including methods for assessing and identifying potential champions. They evaluated athletes for strength and flexibility because both are essential to the power required in Olympic lifting. They also analyzed the athletes' body lever ratios. Some are more efficient than others and knowing them allowed coaches to make adjustments to the athlete's technique to improve lifting capacity.

In the first part of this chapter, I provide instructions for evaluating flexibility. In the second part, I discuss body lever ratios and how they affect one's lifting. You will learn how to assess your own ratios and some tips for compensating for less than perfect ones. This information will shed light on your potential but still leave something to the unknown, that magical and elusive quality that can't be measured.

As an Olympic-style lifter, you probably know that champion Olympic lifters are coordinated, flexible and strong. The combination of these three factors permits the speed and power necessary to the sport. This sometimes surprises people. Though they expect weightlifters to be strong, few realize that successful lifters possess remarkable flexibility. In fact, tight, constricted muscle is incapable of the quickness that the Olympic lifts require.

Before we begin the flexibility measurements, let's do one measurement that will give you an idea of how fit you really are.

The Vertical Jump Measurement

Olympic-style weightlifting might be described as jumping while holding a very heavy bar. No surprise, then, that I recommend measuring an athlete's vertical jump. This test is a general measure of one's physical condition and it is a valuable baseline measurement. There are three steps to it.

First, measure your vertical reach by standing perpendicular to a wall with one shoulder touching it. Raise the arm closest to the wall, reach as high as you can and touch the wall. (When reaching, be sure to keep the shoulders level. There is a tendency to lift the shoulder to extend the reach. Resist this urge.) Chalk on your fingertips will help you mark the spot where your longest finger touches the wall. Measure from the floor to the chalk mark. This is your *reach*.

Second, resume the same position in the same place. Because you want to jump as high as possible, jump as efficiently as you can. You may swing the arm closest to the wall or you may pump the arm straight upward. The idea is to achieve as much height as possible while jumping vertically.

Before taking this measurement, warm up by doing something cardiovascular for five to ten minutes, stretch briefly and then take three or four practice jumps. Put some chalk on your fingers so you can see where you're touching the wall with your reach and jumps.

In the third step, when you are ready, take a short dip, spring up, jump and touch the wall as high as you can. Again, chalk on your fingertips will leave a mark for measurement. The difference between how high you can reach and how high you can jump and touch is your *vertical jump*. Your objective is to jump as high as you can. Don't worry about technique, just jump high.

We find this measurement very useful. Jumping is a basic skill that most people can do well without having done much of it. In most cases, learning the skill is not a factor. We are not testing a specific skill, but an innate and developed ability of hip and leg power. Give yourself three tries and compare your measurement against Chart 1.

Flexibility Measurements

Good flexibility is essential to Olympic lifting. Efficient lifting demands it. Flexibility permits the lifter to recruit power and speed from the muscles, and both are required to raise the bar from the floor and then pull quickly under it into a split or squat. You must be able to come out of the squat with speed, as well. Finally, there is the critical speed of the jerk. None of these movements are possible without good flexibility.

You can get a picture of your flexibility by taking a few simple measurements. No matter what your level of experience or ability, this information will help you train wisely and well. Many factors contribute to an athlete's success, some of which defy measurement. Nonetheless, certain tests can light the way.

For accurate measurements, I recommend a simple tool called a goniometer. It provides an objective way to measure your flexibility, and it's accurate, quick, and easy. By taking these measurements in the beginning, you will have baseline measurements that will allow you to document your progress.

Directions for taking ankle and back thigh flexibility measurements follow. I also discuss measurements of shoulder flexibility in various ranges of motion.

Men and Boys	Age								
	8-9	10-11	12-13	14-15	16-17	18-20	21-25	26-30	31-35
Excellent	12	13	15	17	21	24	26	24	23
Good	10-11	12	13-14	15-16	19-20	22-23	24-25	22-23	21-22
Satisfactory	7-9	9-11	10-12	12-14	16-18	19-21	20-23	21-21	17-20
Fair	5-6	7-8	8-9	10-11	14-15	17-18	18-19	18-19	15-16
Poor	4	6	7	9	13	16	17	17	14
Men and Boys	36-40	41-45	46-50	51-55	56-60	61-65	66-70	71-75	76-80
Excellent	22	21	20	18	17	16	15	14	13
Good	21	20-21	18-19	17	15-16	14-15	13-14	12-13	11-12
Satisfactory	16-20	16-19	14-17	13-16	12-14	11-13	10-12	9-11	8-10
Fair	15	15	12-13	11-12	11	9-10	9	8	7
Poor	14	14	11	10	10	8	8	7	6
Women and Girls	8-9	10-11	12-13	14-15	16-17	18-20	21-25	26-30	31-35
Excellent	10	11	13	15	17	18	19	18	17
Good	8-9	10	11-12	13-14	15-16	16-17	17-18	16-17	15-16
Satisfactory	5-7	8-9	8-10	10-12	11-14	12-15	13-16	12-15	11-14
Fair	3-4	6-7	7	8-9	9-10	10-11	12	11	10
Poor	2	5	6	7	8	9	11	10	9
Women and Girls	36-40	41-45	46-50	51-55	58-60	61-65	66-70	71-75	76-80
Excellent	16	15	14	13	12	11	10	9	8
Good	14-15	13-14	12-13	11-12	11	10	9	8	7
Satisfactory	11-13	10-12	9-11	8-10	9-10	8-9	8	7	6
Fair	10	9	8	7	8	7	7	6	5
Poor	9	8	7	6	7	6	6	5	4

Chart 1. Hip and Leg Power: Using Standing Vertical Jump and Reach

Ankle

We look at ankle flexibility first because the whole body rocks on the ankle joint. When your ankle is flexible, your body has better leverage for propulsion, which is the basis of your lifts. Good ankle flexibility allows your body to assume the most mechanically efficient position, at the right time.

The ankle joint is special because improving its flexibility can be a challenge. It is controlled by a relatively small muscle mass, and there is a lot of fibrous tissue where the gastrocnemius muscle tapers into the Achilles tendon. Fibrous tissue doesn't stretch very much. Also, the articulation of bones in the lower leg, the tibia and fibula, into the bones of the foot, the talus, can greatly restrict the gain of flexibility in the joint. When bone restricts bone, muscle and tissue flexibility is superfluous. If you are young enough, you can have this articulation of bone widened and thus allow for more flexibility gain. A good podiatrist or orthopedic surgeon can do it with a hammer and chisel, but this is a little extreme.

To measure ankle flexibility, find a level surface between ten and fifteen inches off the floor. A low table can work. At my gym, we use a plyometric box.

Ask the subject to place their bare foot on the box surface. It is best if the shin and knee are clearly visible. You are viewing the ankle and knee in profile and are working at the subject's side.

The baseline, marked on the goniometer, will be lined up along the edge of the box, which also aligns the baseline with the sole of the foot. In a neutral position, the tibia, or shin, will be in a straight up-and-down, or perpendicular, position relative to the sole of the foot. This is the 0 degree measurement on the goniometer. Position the goniometer's measuring arm so that it crosses through the mid-point of the ankle joint, from the box surface to the knee. The endpoint of the line will be the mid-point of the knee cap. Try to visualize the position of the tibia, or shin bone, and align the arm of the goniometer with it.

Next, we will measure ankle flexibility. With the foot still on the box, the subject flexes the ankle to bring the shin forward and the knee downward toward the surface of the box. The knee will be deeply bent and overhang the foot. The heel must remain in contact with the box surface. If it rises, even slightly, you are no longer measuring ankle flexibility. The subject may lean their chest against the thigh to provide further pressure. It will be obvious when the subject can flex the ankle no further.

If the neutral position is 0 degrees, by flexing the ankle and bringing the shin forward, we are moving the angle of the shin toward 90 degrees. No one will achieve 90 degrees, but this provides the range of measurement for this joint. As Chart 2 indicates, an average ankle measurement is between 35 and 43 degrees.

Back of Thigh or Hamstring

We measure back thigh, or hamstring flexibility, because the hamstring serves the knee and hip joints. Specifically, the hamstrings act to extend the knees and hips, and in the Olympic lifts, this extension must be quick and powerful. Only a flexible back thigh can respond with the necessary quickness.

To take this measurement, you will again need the goniometer. Have the subject recline on a flat bench, and place one foot on the bench so the lower spine is in a neutral position. Raise the knee of the other leg so that the thigh is perpendicular to the floor. This will create a right angle at the hip joint. Now raise the shin so that it is parallel to the floor, forming a right angle at the back of the knee.

Place the hinge of the goniometer against the "hinge" of the knee joint, and align the baseline with the femur, or thigh bone. Align the measuring arm with the tibia, or shin bone. It may be necessary to adjust the positions of the shin and knee to obtain a true right angle at the knee. This is the starting position.

Have your subject slowly extend the leg by raising the foot toward the ceiling, hinging off the knee while keeping the thigh stationary. The ideal position is a straight knee with the leg perpendicular to the floor, but this is rare. Most people cannot fully straighten their knee in this position.

Observe the position of the thigh! Do not let the thigh drop downward toward the bench as the knee extends. And verify the position of the hip on the bench! Some people tend to lift their hip to help extend their leg. Dropping the thigh and lifting the hip are clear indicators of back thigh tightness.

When the subject's knee is fully extended, stabilize the thigh with one hand, and press the calf gently with the other hand to straighten the knee a little more. Remember, the neutral position is 0 degrees so the measurement you take will typically be in the range of 60 to 90 plus degrees. See Chart 2 for norms.

Shoulder Flexion

We also measure shoulder flexion with the goniometer. When the bar is in the overhead position, as in the jerk or the finish position of the snatch, you're striving for a secure bone-on-bone lock between the humerus and the glenoid fossa. When the bar is held directly overhead, the muscles work only enough to balance and stabilize it. This will conserve energy.

To measure shoulder flexibility, you must locate the spot on the subject's shoulder against which to place the goniometer's hinge. To find this point, ask the subject to stand and raise the hand toward the ceiling. Begin at the elbow, and feel for this point by running your hand down the side of the arm. Just below shoulder level, your fingers will slide over the bulge of the deltoid and then hit a small concavity. You will feel the point where the deltoid and latissimus muscles converge. This is where you place the hinge of the goniometer.

The subject should recline on a flat bench, head supported by the bench, and if comfortable, feet flat on it, too. Raise the arm perpendicular to the bench and spine. Align the baseline of the goniometer with the bench, and place the hinge over the concavity you located, just under the deltoid. The extended arm is at 90 degrees on the goniometer.

Ask the subject to drop the arm back, away from the chest, toward the floor and in line with the body. You may gently press the arm downward to complete the full range of the subject's shoulder flexibility. Be gentle.

Again, the shoulder angle when the arm is upright is 90 degrees to the body. The flexed shoulder is greater than 90 degrees, usually in a range of roughly 130 to 180 degrees.

The shoulder joint is a miracle of engineering and capable of motion on many planes. Olympic lifting calls upon the shoulder to move very freely. Internal rotation and external rotation are important parts of lifting efficiently, which is so much a part of the Olympic style.

Shoulder Internal Rotation

We can also assess the internal rotation of the shoulder. With sufficient internal rotation of the shoulder, it is easier to elevate the scapula, or shoulder blade. This will add significant height to your pull, and the bar can be raised higher.

To assess a shoulder's internal rotation range of motion, have the subject stand straight, with chest lifted and arms relaxed. Take one arm and position it so that the elbow can bend at a right angle and the forearm is parallel to the floor behind the subject's back. The forearm will rest at waist height.

This, alone, may be difficult for the subject and would immediately indicate low flexibility in the shoulder's internal rotation flexibility. If the subject is not uncomfortable in this position, slowly and gently, raise the subject's forearm upward while stabilizing the shoulder with your other hand.

If your subject tilts forward from the waist, or rounds the upper back to raise the arm higher, the shoulder has reached its maximum rotation. An arm elevation of a few inches indicates a healthy degree of flexibility.

Shoulder External Rotation

Good flexibility here relates to shoulder flexion. Both are necessary. One without the other is incomplete. To assess your subject's range of motion, he or she should stand very straight with the upper arms pressed tightly to the side and ribs. Have the subject bend one arm so that the elbow is at a 90-degree angle, and the forearm is parallel to the floor. This is the start position.

Now, the subject should slowly open that arm outward and away from the mid-line of the body, as though the arm is a door bring opened outward. If the start position is 0 degrees, we consider an open arm measurement of between 75 degrees and 90 degrees a healthy range.

To conclude, with proper training, most people can improve their flexibility significantly. Though it is true that flexibility is somewhat genetically determined, even the least flexible among us can improve and most can score within the "Satisfactory" range or above. In the beginning of a stretching, we find that two or three degrees of flexibility can be gained every six weeks, until a near limit is reached. After that, the gain is slower and harder. Nonetheless, every increment of improvement helps.

Flexibility	Ankle	Hamstring	Shoulder Flexion	Shoulder Internal Rotation	Shoulder External Rotation
Excellent	50+	92+	182+	90+	90+
Above avg	44-49	89-91	179-181	85-89	88-89
Norm	35-43	84-88	175-178	75-84	84-87
Below avg	29-34	80-83	171-174	70-74	79-83
Poor	-28	-79	-170	-69	-78

Chart 2. Flexibility Norms (degrees)

Body Segment Proportions and Measurement

As a lifter, you may already understand that Olympic lifting is physics in action. It largely comes down to levers and fulcrums and ratios. Even if you never read the text in school, you are learning physics every time you practice a lift.

Champion Olympic lifters tend to have particular body proportions that are especially suited to the demands of the sport. "Pocket Hercules" Naim Süleymanoglu has a long back but otherwise exhibits classic proportions. Interestingly, so does his former arch- rival, Valerios Leonidis. Their contemporary Pyrros Dimas, does, too. Going back a little further in time, David Rigert, Anatoly Pisarenko, Yuri Vardanyan and Vasili Alexeev also possessed powerful lever ratios that they maximized with amazing coordination and timing. Only a lucky few of us have the perfect lifter's body; however, there are ways to compensate by adjusting your lifting form and maximizing the efficiency of your own body type.

In this section, you will learn how to measure body segments and what these measurements suggest about improving your Olympic lifting "physics." When you know the proportions of specific body segments, you can develop variations in lifting styles to bolster less favorable leverages. Having a good grasp of your body proportions and levers also will aid you in identifying which muscles you should strengthen.

The specifications that follow are taken from data I have collected since 1973 and represent a total of 721 lifters, including some of the best in the world. The segments measured were chosen in consultation with numerous sports professionals and weightlifting coaches. The measuring points are easily located. If the measurements are off by a small margin, do not be concerned. These small errors are constant in all measurements and should not significantly affect results. Please note, these proportions are only valid for these measuring points. If you use other points, do not compare the different sets of measurements.

Upper Arm Length to Whole Arm Length

To measure the length of your upper arm, measure from the acromion process of the scapula, the bony tip of the shoulder, straight down (not around the bulge of the deltoid) to the lateral epicondyle of the humerus, or the bony knob easily found on the outside of your bent elbow. The length of your whole arm is measured from the acromion process to the styloid process of the radius, or wrist bone.

An upper arm measurement that is *more than 56 percent of total arm length* is longer than the average for the 721 lifters I assessed. This means it will be harder to hold the bar at your shoulders in the clean. With your relatively long upper arm, the bar rests lower on the clavicle. To compensate, point your elbows outward, thus reducing the length of the lever that is your upper arm. Some lifters prefer a narrow grip, but a narrower grip can make the lockout in the jerk less stable and more difficult. Try a wider grip because it is easier to finish out.

If you have long upper arms, it will be helpful to develop pressing strength within the range of the shoulder and the nose. This helps develop the power needed when the bar leaves the shoulders in the upward pump of the jerk. Work on the pressing movement from the top of the hairline to full extension. This will help develop the power needed to push under the bar and lock out well.

Shoulder flexibility is important for Olympic lifting, especially if you have long arms. It will greatly improve your leverage. This enables the bar to rest high on the clavicle and set easily into the groove at the top of the jerk.

Arm Length to Total Body Length

The method for measuring arm length is described in the previous section. Your total body length is measured from the fifth cervical vertebra to the medial malleolus of the tibia, or the ankle bone. Your weight should be equally distributed on both feet when measuring.

An arm length *more than 38 percent of the total body measurement* is longer than our average from the 721 lifters I studied. There are predictable consequences of a longer arm to body ratio. This time the consequences tend to be positive. Your hips will be higher when grabbing the bar in the start position, which means better thigh and hip leverage for lifting the bar off the floor. It throws your body's center of gravity forward so you're closer in line with the center of gravity of the bar, which is good. Your shoulders are also more in front of the bar, which is good.

There can be downsides with longer arm to body ratios, too. With this long lever, any error in the direction of the bar will be magnified. It might be hard to control the direction of the bar, and it can get away from you. There are two methods for controlling the bar's trajectory. One is to curl your wrists so that your palms roll under the wrists slightly. The second method is to keep your elbows out to the side, and lifted upward, rather than pulling the elbows back. If these methods do not help control the bar, try using a wider grip, which shortens the lever and minimizes any error in the bar's direction. Avoid a very wide grip because this reduces the leverage advantage of relatively long arms.

An arm length *less than 38 percent of your total body measurement* is shorter than our average. Your hips will be lower when you grab the bar, so poor leverage is likely as the bar comes off the floor. You will tend to shift your bodyweight back onto your heels, which leads to pulling from your heels instead of from the full length of your foot. Finally, your shoulders will tend to get in back of the bar.

To compensate for these disadvantages, use a wider grip, or try to raise your hips by moving closer to the bar with a narrow foot stance. If you develop greater hip and leg strength, your compensation will be more effective. Exercises for the lower third of your thigh are especially important because this portion of the thigh, which is so important in getting a full hip extension, usually is underdeveloped in lifters with long upper thighs.

Thigh Length to Leg Length

Your thigh is measured from the greater trochanter of the femur, or the prominent hip bone found on the outside of the hip, to the lowest part of the lateral epicondyle of the femur. The latter is located easily by feeling for the knob on the outside of the knee joint. Your leg length is measured from the greater trochanter to the lateral malleolus of the fibula.

A thigh measurement *less than 56 percent of your leg length measurement* is shorter than our average. In this situation, you have good leverage for leg and hip power because the end of the lever, your hips, is closer to the bar. Your center of gravity is comparatively forward, bringing it closer to the center of gravity of the bar. A short thigh is also advantageous for jerking leverage. If there is a disadvantage to a short thigh, it might be a temptation to drop the hips, because you feel so much leg power throughout most of the range of motion.

A thigh measurement *more than 56 percent of your leg length measurement* is longer than our average. Because lifting involves so much hip and leg power, it is imperative to reduce the lever of your long upper leg. With your long thigh, your center of gravity is further from the bar and is far behind your shoulders. The weight attachment to the long lever of your thigh is so far from the fulcrum, and so far from the bar's center of gravity, that hip and leg power are greatly reduced. As your center of gravity is so far back, you will tend to lift off your heels and your shoulders will shift behind the bar. This reduces power and directs the bar outward and to the front.

To reduce the lever of your long thigh, you want to increase ankle, hip and quadriceps flexibility. This will help you shift your hips forward. Try raising your hips so that your thigh is slightly above a horizontal position, relative to the platform. Not only does this enhance leverage for the muscles of your hips and legs, it also shortens the lever of the thigh. You might try adjusting your grip. A narrower grip on the bar also can help to raise the level of the hips.

The position of your feet can make a difference, too. A narrower stance will shorten the depth of your dip for the jerk. Less depth on the dip creates a more sudden stop, thus calling upon the stretch reflex in the leg muscles. The abrupt stop can induce more bend in the bar, creating what is called a bar whip.

With a longer thigh, your hips and legs require more work, with greater intensity, in both the pull and jerk. Extra strength training for the lower third of your thigh is especially important.

Back Length to Total Body Length

The length of the back is measured from the fifth cervical to the fifth lumbar vertebra. The method of total body length measurement is described above.

A back length measurement *less than 40 percent of your body length measurement* is shorter than our average. Because pulling and jerking require so much hip and leg power, a shorter than average back allows a more direct transfer of power to the bar. That means good leverage. The shoulders will remain slightly in front of the bar for much of the lift, which means that the lever of the hips and back is stronger. Full hip extension is easier because the upper body barely overhangs the bar. The muscles of your hips and legs have a short lever (the upper back) to bring through a narrower arc.

A back length measurement *more than 40 percent of your body length measurement* is longer than our average. Consequently, there is more of an overhang for much of the lift, and you need more strength in your lower back. The scoop (shift, for second knee bend) is harder because your hip and leg muscles must bring this long lever (upper back) through a wider arc. You can do several things to compensate. You may want to adjust your starting position to stand a little farther from the bar. You could adopt a wider foot stance to bring the upper body farther back. You might try a wider grip on the bar to reduce the overhang of the shoulders caused by the long back.

In my observations, lifters with long backs tend to be good snatchers. It is my opinion that because the snatch weight is lighter when compared to the clean, the long upper body lever acts as a whip. Or maybe the longer distance between the floor and the finish position in the snatch allows the back more of a whip effect.

The clean is different. The weight of the bar in the clean is so heavy that the long upper body cannot act like a whip. The whip is actually dead-ended because of the magnitude of the weight.

To conclude this discussion of body proportions, note that the lifter with short upper arms, long whole arms, short thighs and short back will have better leverage than a lifter whose proportions deviate from this. In spite of the importance of leverage, it is not the whole story of lifting. Important qualities such as speed, distance of muscle attachments from the ends of bones, and muscle quality also affect a lifter's "physics." No lifter alive has perfect proportions, and things can be done to modify a leverage disadvantage. Be thankful for the gifts you do have. Know your leverage strengths and shortcomings, and then work within this framework.

Notes

2

Making Use of Stress

To understand the science behind the training schedules provided in this book, it's necessary to talk briefly about the work of Hans Selye (1907–1982). A giant in the field of medicine, Hans Selye researched and wrote extensively on the subject of stress. His theories have influenced numerous disciplines, including medicine, psychology and sport science. The work of this famed Austrian-born physician covered decades.

Selye was a pioneer in the study of the body's responses to stress. In 1936 he introduced his "General Adaptation Syndrome," theory and with it, launched a new way of thinking about how the body accommodates and adapts to stress. He describes it as a response, "Stress is the nonspecific response of the body to any demand, whether it is caused by, or results in, pleasant or unpleasant conditions…Stress is not necessarily undesirable. It all depends on how you take it…The stress reaction, like energy consumption, may have good or bad effects."

Selye lived and worked in Montreal, and in 1981, while giving a coaching clinic there, I had the opportunity to meet him. I was honored that this very busy man would share a couple of hours with me over a cup of coffee.

Selye's research revealed that stress is essential to change. His work identified the fact that unless one is pushed or coaxed, change will not likely take place. Substitute the word "progress" for "change," and you will see where this is leading. In light of Selye's findings, training methods have been developed that systematically induce stress to coax the body into progressing.

Selye identified three stages of stress response. The first he called the alarm stage, during which stress is initiated, and the body learns to accommodate the stressor. This can last from 4 to 12 weeks. The second stage, which he named the resistance stage, is marked by complete adaptation to the stress induced. This is a period of peak condition and can last from 3 to 6 weeks. The third and final stage, or exhaustion stage, is marked by the loss of peak condition and total exhaustion.

We now know that each of these stages can be identified through specific chemical changes in the body, changes that are easily monitored. The two most reliable and easily monitored responses are blood levels of cortisol and white blood cell counts. Levels of cortisol, a product of the adrenal cortex, rise during the alarm stage. They remain constant during the resistance stage and then drop during the exhaustion stage. Measurements of eosinophil, a white blood cell, rise with the exhaustion stage.

Selye was not writing for weightlifting per se, but the basic principles he outlined have been very important to the sport. The three stages of the *General Adaptation Syndrome* have corollaries in lifting that are called the preparation phase (alarm stage), the contest phase (resistance stage) and re-adaptation phase (exhaustion stage.)

Competitive weightlifters understand that competitions provide incentive for hard training. To achieve peak condition, successful lifters schedule their training to peak for specific meets, so it is frustrating to train hard for competition only to experience a drop in performance just before the event. Applying Selye's theory to your own training can help you to time your peak, understand your fatigue and remain strong.

I had been convinced of the importance of this science while doing my research in East Berlin. I observed coaches taking blood from the ears of their swimmers each day. They were testing the athletes' blood for levels of eosinophil and cortisol. Training programs were adjusted daily on the basis of this blood analysis, and partly because of this, the East German team had the fastest swimmers in the world. After the disappointing performance of American athletes at the 1972 Olympics, it became apparent that our training programs had to change. As coaching coordinator for the Olympic Weightlifting team, I ordered similar, periodic blood tests for the lifters. I was the first national coach to use them.

A very good illustration of different training phases took place at one of the Olympic-style training camps I held in Santa Fe, New Mexico. I introduced participants to a number of new ideas; perhaps the least popular was the one about a lab technician taking blood samples every other day.

One of the lifters attending my camp was a teenage weightlifting phenomenon prone to bouts of boredom and fatigue. He held all the US records for his age group, and by the age of 16, he was incurring serious injuries rare in someone so young. His coach wanted me to help him understand the need to adjust training intensity according to Selye's phases.

When I met JF, he was frustrated because his training had not been going well. He had been struggling for the previous three months. For two weeks before camp, he had trained lightly because of pain. Now he was relatively pain free and wanted to train all the time. On the first night, JF was given the week's schedule and noticed we didn't lift until mid-morning. He asked if he could train before breakfast and also during the two-hour lunch break at noon. He wanted to train after dinner, too.

When JF came into camp, his cortisol and eosinophil levels were in the normal range. We drew blood every second day for the remaining two weeks. By the third draw, JF's cortisol levels started to drop dramatically, and his eosinophil levels started to climb. In just six days, his body showed symptoms of overtraining. He was extremely fatigued and irritable. He entered the exhaustion stage that quickly. I showed him the results of training too hard. What a perfect set up! The results made believers of them all (Chart 3).

Lifter	Cortisol µ/dl		Eosinophil cµ/mm		Comments
	First Day	Last Day	First Day	Last Day	
PD	16.9	17.6	200	177	Trained as directed
RF	16.0	12.3	11	178	Trained harder than directed
KG	12.4	14.4	66	54	Trained as directed
PH	12.6	10.5	10	260	Trained harder than directed
LS	23.1	28.4	78	52	Trained as directed
PS	16.0	19.4	115	86	Trained as directed
JF	12.6	6.5	52	276	Trained way too hard; Was advised not to, but did

Normal ranges: Cortisol: 5-28 µg/dl

When body is meeting stress, this value goes UP
When body not meeting stress, this goes DOWN

Eosinophil: 50-250 cµ/mm

When body is meeting stress, this goes DOWN
When body not meeting stress, this value goes UP

Chart 3. Blood Analysis

Notes

3

**Let's
Play
Weightlifting**

really value play. I am not alone. Numerous studies have shown that an atmosphere of play makes work pleasurable and that important learning takes place within the context of play. We continue to learn during our lives through the play in which we engage. Sport is an obvious example. Sportsmanship, team work, concentration, and goal setting are honed through play, even as we age. The more fun you have with anything you undertake, the more successful you will be. This holds especially true for the hard play of weight training.

When I was teaching, coaching and researching in Japan, I learned to speak Japanese. They had an expression for having fun in individual sports. In the literal translation from Japanese, one says, "*I am going to play...*" weightlifting or running, javelin, wrestling or boxing. For people to stay with things they do voluntarily, and to enjoy things like going to work or to exercise, there must be an element of play. Variety is a big piece of it.

Variety is an important aspect of my systems for developing strength and power. Meaningful variety helps relieve the routine and restores a quality of play to your workouts. By practicing elements of Olympic lifting, whether with barbells or dumbbells, we get meaningful change within the exercise and introduce a play element to our strenuous workouts.

Usually, between 8 and 18 repetitions are recommended in a barbell or dumbbell exercise. Chart 4 offers 30 different, meaningful combinations that you might find fun and stimulating. Many of these combinations use shortened ranges of motion such as jerks, cleans, or snatches from the thigh, and clean or snatch dead lifts. A shortened range of motion makes it easier to maintain your form as you perform a number of repetitions. This will help develop your Olympic lifting technique and power.

In most of the exercises that follow, you will move from the least favorable mechanical leverage to the most favorable, as the motions are combined into a meaningful progression. Each repetition is high quality because we pick up a leverage advantage through the course of the progression.

Keep in mind that the quality of everyone's leverage is a little different, so you may need to modify the number of repetitions you do. Don't worry, because one or two repetitions, one way or the other, will not make a difference. If you run out of gas too soon, reduce the number of repetitions. If you modify the exercises, remember that as you pick up mechanical leverage throughout the progressions, the exercises should get easier. Adjust accordingly. You may use either the squat or split style in the exercises. In a few, you will see that the power style is recommended, which means catching the bar without splitting or squatting, but with straight knees.

Use these exercises during the re-adaptation or strength phases of your training program. Weightlifting play is beneficial for Olympic-style lifters of all ability levels.

1) SNATCH: 2 high thigh; POWER CLEAN: 3 floor, 4-5 thigh
2) SNATCH: 1 power floor, 2 floor, 2-3 knee height, 4-5 high thigh
3) SNATCH: 2 power floor, 3 floor, 3-4 knee height, 4-5 high thigh
4) SNATCH: 2 floor; CLEAN: 3 power knee height, 4-5 high thigh
5) SNATCH: 1 floor, 2 knee height, 3 high thigh; PULLS: 2 floor, 3 knee height, 4-5 high thigh
6) SNATCH: 1-2 power floor, 2-3 floor, 1 power knee, 2 knee height, 2-3 power high thigh
7) SNATCH: 1 floor, 2 high thigh; SNATCH PULL: 2 floor; CLEAN: 3 floor, 4-5 high thigh
8) SNATCH: 1 floor, 2 high thigh; CLEAN: 3 floor; CLEAN PULL: 4 knee height, 5 high thigh
9) SNATCH PULL: 3 floor; SNATCH: 1 high thigh; CLEAN: 2-3 floor, 3-4 knee height
10) SNATCH PULL: 2 floor, 3 knee height, 4-5 high thigh
1) CLEAN: 3 floor, 3-4 knee height, 4-5 high thigh
2) CLEAN: 2 power floor, 2 floor, 2-3 knee height, 3-4 high thigh
3) CLEAN: 2 power floor, 2-3 knee height, 3-5 high thigh
4) CLEAN: 1 power floor, 2 power high thigh, 2 floor, 2-3 knee height, 3-4 high thigh
5) CLEAN: 3-4 power floor; SNATCH DEAD LIFT: 1; SNATCH: 1 high thigh; SNATCH PULL: 4-5 high thigh
6) CLEAN: 2 floor, 2-3 knee height, 4-5 high thigh; PULL: 3-5 floor
7) CLEAN: 1-2 power floor, 2-3 floor, 1 power knee, 2 knee, 2-3 power high thigh
8) CLEAN: 1 floor, 1-2 knee height, 2-3 high thigh; CLEAN PULL: 2-3 floor; 3-4 knee height, 4-5 high thigh
9) CLEAN: 1 floor, 2-3 high thigh; CLEAN PULL: 3-4 floor, 4-5 knee height, 4-5 high thigh
10) CLEAN PULL: 1 floor, 2-3 knee height, 4-5 high thigh
1) JERK: from stand-toss: 2 chin, 3 eyebrow; POWER JERK: 4; SPLIT: 5
2) JERK: from stand-toss: 2 eyebrow; POWER JERK: 3; SPLIT: 5-6
3) JERK: from stand, any combination: 3 power, 5-6 split; 4 power, 8 split
4) JERK: same as #1 only from back
5) JERK: same as #2 only from back
6) JERK: same as #3 only from back
7) JERK: from stand, any combination: 3 front, 5 back; 4 front, 10 back
8) JERK: from stand: 4-5; SNATCH PULL: 3-5 floor; CLEAN: 1 floor, 1-2 knee height, 3-4 high thigh
9) JERK: from stand: 4-5; SNATCH DEAD LIFT: 1; SNATCH PULL: 2-3 knee height, 3-4 high thigh; CLEAN: 3-4 floor
10) JERK: from stand: 2 front, 3 back; CLEAN: 1 floor, 1-2 knee height, 3-4 high thigh

Chart 4. Let's Play Weightlifting

Notes

4

Competition, Classes and Training Phases

At one time, lifters were divided into classes on the basis of ability and experience, as expressed by the total weight lifted, which is the sum of their best snatch and best clean and jerk. The classes were the following: 1) Class IV, 2) Class III, 3) Class II, 4) Class I, 5) master, and 6) elite (Chart 5). I use the classes in this chapter because the system provides a helpful structure for our discussion.

Men						
Wt. Class (kg)	Class IV	Class III	Class II	Class I	Master	Elite
56	108 and below	148	163	193	253	268
62	122 and below	170	175	208	273	288
69	128 and below	175	195	230	300	318
77	138 and below	190	205	243	314	335
85	140 and below	190	215	255	333	353
94	148 and below	203	220	260	340	360
105	150 and below	207	233	275	360	380
105+	155 and below	215	253	298	385	410

Women						
Wt. Class (kg)	Class IV	Class III	Class II	Class I	Master	Elite
48	68 and below	93	103	120	157	165
53	78 and below	105	110	130	173	180
58	83 and below	115	118	140	180	190
63	88 and below	120	123	145	193	203
69	88 and below	120	128	150	200	205
75	90 and below	123	130	155	200	213
75+	98 and below	135	138	163	218	230

Chart 5. Determine your Class Category by Total Kilograms Lifted

Novice, or Class IV, lifters will always make good progress because all training in the early weeks of lifting yields greater strength. This is logical because a novice athlete's training rarely approaches their maximum potential. To continue making progress and remain injury free, though, you need an effective training structure. The correct training system will assist your advancement to the higher ranked classes. There is no reason for a focused and hard-working lifter to become bogged down in any single class. By training under a sound system, you will be coaxed into greater improvement.

I want to stress that the work you do in the gym is only part of your development. You must become familiar with competition. It is an important learning tool for lifters of all ability levels. Get used to it. Learn to enjoy it. The adrenaline rush you may experience in competition will affect your lifts in surprising and wonderful ways. Competition will bring out your best effort and also provide a framework for all your training.

Compete whenever you have the opportunity, even if you are at a low point in your training cycle. There is no reason not to, and it is a proven strategy in other countries. It is possible that a contest will catch you unexpectedly at your best. In this case, don't hold back. Treat the contest as a workout, and if the weights feel light, go for records.

There are more competitions for lower category lifters than for higher category lifters. A lower category lifter can compete more often because their learning curve is steeper, and they can tolerate the training appropriate to their level of development. This is reflected in the charts below.

A high category lifter has probably participated in many competitions. He or she is a veteran and needs to spend more time training at higher intensities. Such a lifter cannot expect to peak more than three or four times in a year, so it is likely you will enter fewer competitions in which you'll compete to win.

The entire preparation, contest and re-adaptation cycle for an elite lifter takes 16 weeks. This can be divided into an 8-week preparation phase, a 6-week contest phase and a 2-week re-adaptation phase. During the course of a year, a lifter can complete three cycles (three 16-week periods), with a 4-week vacation (Chart 6).

It is not always possible to peak at precisely the correct time, but it is possible to understand why. And you can come close. Every competition is an opportunity to learn more about yourself and your sport.

Preparation Phase

The preparation phase is the stage in your training during which you achieve peak condition. It is important to know that in this phase you are lifting while tired much of the time. You train to the point of tiredness and then train more. You are actually doing more work at higher intensities than you will during the next phase, called the contest phase. Training tired during the preparation phase has been a successful practice by the East Europeans. This approach is not limited to weightlifting. Sports such as track and field and swimming have used it for years.

You will be tired because you are doing more work, work as measured by actual time spent per type of exercise. This approach was adopted by the East Europeans and the Japanese. Standards are adjusted for each weightlifting class. (Times recommended here do not include the one or two minute rest between lifts.) The key principle is that time is scheduled for drills according to each drill's importance. This way, each workout is as productive as possible. Many professional football and basketball teams train in this manner, too.

Contest Phase

The contest phase starts when you reach peak condition and remain there for competition. The time allotted to training is reduced. You train until you are tired and then no more. Workouts are short and sweet. Of course, they may not seem that much shorter, but the little bit of easing off allows freshness. Too much easing, though, and you lose the edge towards which you have been building.

Readaptation Phase

In the readaptation phase, you come down off a peak, maintain good weightlifting condition and ease into another cycle of preparation. This is a very important phase because your body needs to recuperate. The adrenals have been functioning at a very high level for weeks, and they cannot continue such high output. Remember Selye. If you go from competition immediately back into a preparation phase, the adrenals cannot recover. After 7 to 18 weeks of preparation, they will require a period of recuperation. Without it, their output cannot return to normal, and eosinophil counts will drop from the unremitting stress. It is physically impossible to maintain peak performance at this point.

There are two methods of training in the readaptation phase. In the first method, choose a weight within 50 to 60 percent of your best, and do four to six repetitions and as many sets as possible within the time allotted. You are permitted only one minute of rest between sets. In the second method, choose a weight within 40 to 50 percent of your best, and do four to six repetitions, going from exercise to exercise with no rest. The exercises can be grouped so that the time allotted to each exercise grouping is covered, and the exercises are placed so they do not fatigue any one muscle group.

Remember that in the readaptation phase, you come down off a peak, maintain good conditioning and ease into another cycle of preparation. By reducing the intensity of your workout, you allow the adrenal glands to recuperate. Either of the two methods just described help accomplish this, Workouts should be physically refreshing and include enough fast work to be stimulating. At the end of this phase, you will be mentally, physically and emotionally ready to begin the preparation phase of the next cycle.

Vacation

A vacation really should be called active rest. A vacation is a complete change of living habits that allows you to feel fresh for the upcoming training sessions. The theory is to have fun actively. It is taken for granted that athletes like movement, so when you go on "vacation," have fun with movement. This way you have fun, enjoy a change of pace and maintain your conditioning. All sports qualify as vacation activities. Try basketball, soccer, track and field, paddleball, handball, gymnastics, swimming, bicycling, skiing or ice skating. You can engage in sports everywhere you go. Have fun with them and enjoy the activity. Allow your mind and emotions to rest.

Training Times for Progress

Adaptability is the key to getting the most out of your training. We have only to look at the long, intense, four to six hour training sessions of our top swimmers and wrestlers. They do not start out that way. They follow adaptive training methods of increasing work and intensity. As their bodies adapt, they swim faster or wrestle better.

Most East Europeans train longer than the time presented here. I have adapted their training schedules to something realistic for us. Even so, for some people it will seem like too much time at the gym. Keep at it, anyway. These are general guidelines and can be modified to the needs of individual lifters (Chart 7).

If the training really is too long for you, you may be over reaching for your class. Your body may not be adaptable to this training. If you are such a lifter, try training to the specifications one category below your actual rating. Remember, to lift more weight you must increase your intensity and workload wisely. With systematic training and excellent health habits, you will adapt to more intensity and work.

Class IV
Eight competitions, one every 5 to 6 weeks.
Two phases of four competitions with a vacation between each phase.

#1	#2	#3	#4
1-2 week prep	1-2 week prep	1-2 week prep	1-2 week prep
3 week contest	3 week contest	3 week contest	3 week contest
1 week readapt	1 week readapt	1 week readapt	1 week readapt

About 24 weeks total depending on duration of prep phase

-Vacation-

#5	#6	#7	#8
Same as #1	Same as #2	Same as #3	Same as #4

Class III
Six competitions, one every 7 to 8 weeks.
Two phases of three competitions with a vacation between each phase.

#1	#2	#3
3 week prep	2-3 week prep	2-3 week prep
4 week contest	4 week contest	4 week contest
1 week readapt	1 week readapt	1 week readapt

About 23 weeks total depending on duration of prep phase

-Vacation-

#4	#5	#6
Same as #1	Same as #2	Same as #3

Class II
Five competitions, one every 9 to 10 weeks.
One phase of five competitions with a vacation at the end.

#1	#2	#3	#4	#5
5 week prep	5 week prep	5 week prep	5 week prep	5 week prep
4 week contest	4 week contest	4 week contest	4 week contest	4 week contest
1 week readapt	1 week readapt	1 week readapt	1 week readapt	1 week readapt

About 50 weeks total

-Vacation-

Class I
Four competitions, one every 12 weeks in one phase with a vacation at the end.

#1	#2	#3	#4
6 week prep	6 week prep	6 week prep	6 week prep
5 week contest	5 week contest	5 week contest	5 week contest
1 week readapt	1 week readapt	1 week readapt	1 week readapt

About 48 weeks total

-Vacation-

Master and Elite
Three competitions, one every 16 weeks in one phase with a vacation at the end.

#1	#2	#3
8 week prep	8 week prep	8 week prep
6 week contest	6 week contest	6 week contest
2 week readapt	2 week readapt	2 week readapt

About 48 weeks total

-Vacation-

Chart 6. Competitive Cycles and Length of Training Phases by Class

Give yourself every chance of success. Good health habits support your body as it adapts to increasing stress. This means sufficient sleep. It means eating well. It means not smoking. It also means being careful with alcohol. Alcohol affects the enzymatic system, which plays such an important role in assimilating foods. A bottle of beer cuts down on the assimilation of B vitamins for nine days. B vitamins aid in the digestion of proteins, contribute to the formation of red blood cells, and help metabolize carbohydrates to make energy.

Good health habits also include being at peace with yourself and eliminating stress. There is enough emotional stress in training and competing. Adding other outside problems interferes with recovery between workouts.

Phase	Elite	Master	I	II	III	IV
Preparation						
hours/workout	3.0-3.5	2.5-3.0	2.0-2.5	1.75-2.0	1.5-1.75	1.25-1.5
hours/week	15.0-17.5	12.5-15.0	10.0-12.5	8.75-10.0	6.0-7.0	3.75-4.5
sessions/week	5	5	5	5	4	3
Contest						
hours/workout	2.5-3.0	2.0-2.5	1.5-1.75	1.25-1.5	1.0-1.25	1.0-1.25
hours/week	12.5-15.0	10.0-12.5	7.5-8.75	6.25-7.5	4.0-6.0	3.0-3.75
sessions/week	5	5	5	5	4	3
Readaptation						
hours/workout	1.5-1.75	1.5	1.25-1.5	1.0-1.25	0.75-1.0	0.5-0.75
hours/week	7.5-8.75	7.5	6.25-7.25	5.0-6.25	3-4	1.5-2.25
sessions/week	5	5	5	4	3	3
Vacation						
hours/fun period	1	1	1	1	1	1
fun periods/week	5	5	5	4	3	3

Chart 7. Training Times for Classes and Phases

To help organize the countless number of exercises, we group and list related ones. Each is designated as technique oriented (T), power oriented (P) or strength oriented (S).

Snatch Related		Jerk Related	
Type	Exercise	Type	Exercise
T	1. Complete from floor	P	1. Push press
T	2. From knees	P	2. Push up and out
T	3. From mid-thigh	T+P	3. On toes, split/recover
T+P	4. Dead lift to knees	P	4. Push drive
P	5. Power snatch	T	5. Balance
T+P	6. High pull/straight arms	T	6. Jerk/eyes closed
T+P	7. High pull/arms coming out	T	7. Front squat and jerk
T	8. Overhead squat	T	8. Jerk from rack
P+S	9. Isokinetics	P+S	9. Isokinetics
S	10. Eccentric contraction	S	10. Eccentric contraction

Clean Related		Leg Related	
Type	Exercise	Type	Exercise
T	1. Complete from floor	P	1. Front squat
T	2. From knees	P	2. Super killer squat
T	3. From mid-thigh	P	3. Speed squat
T+P	4. Dead lift to knees	P	4. Pre-exhaustion
T+P	5. Power clean	P	5. Back squat (Olympic)
T+P	6. High pull/straight arms	T+P	6. Back squat (pull position)
T+P	7. High pull/arms coming out	P	7. Split squat
T+P	8. Position squat	T+P	8. Olympic clean dead lift
P+S	9. Isokinetics	P+S	9. Isokinetics
S	10. Eccentric contraction	S	10. Eccentric contraction

Chart 8. Exercise Groupings

Remedial Exercises

Remedial exercises promote specialized strengthening in the back, legs and shoulders (Chart 9). They are not practiced for very long or with great intensity. Too much remedial exercise can expose you to injury or overdevelopment, which may lead to injury. The purpose of remedial exercise is to balance the overdevelopment incurred when doing the standard platform drills. Leg curls balance the development of the quads. Bench presses balance the pulls. We do not need big pecs, so we don't have to bench big weights. We want chest strength for general shoulder strength and stability. Seated presses will strengthen the chest and shoulders to prevent injury, and just a few sets at the end of the allotted time period are sufficient.

Legs	Back	Shoulders
1. Leg extension 2. Leg curl 3. Leg push 4. Hack machine 5. Isokinetics	1. Good morning 2. Hyperextension 3. Still leg dead lift 4. ¾ hyperextension 5. Isokinetics 6. Bent knee sit ups	1. Seat press 2. Bench press 3. Behind neck press 4. Stand military press 5. Power snatch to forehead and press out

Chart 9. Remedial Exercises

Exercises Grouped By Training Goals

Exercises are grouped into categories according to specific goals of a workout. Chart 10 is a list of these categories and the number of times per week they are practiced.

Class	Snatch tech	Snatch power	C & J tech	Clean tech	Clean power	Jerk power	Jerk tech	Leg	Back	Shoulder	Total
IV & below	2	1	2	1	1	2	1	2	1	1	14
III	2	2	2	1	2	2	1	2	2	2	18
II	2	2	2	1	2	3	2	3	2	2	21
I	3	3	2	1	3	4	2	3	2	2	25
Master	3	4	2	1	4	5	2	4	2	2	29
Elite	3	5	2	1	5	6	2	5	2	2	33

Chart 10. Exercises Grouped By Training Goals

As you advance through the rankings and improve technique, concentrate on developing strength. The clean and jerk is made up of two separate skills. The two skills are separated for some specialized learning. The number of times various facets of the lifts are practiced per week progresses. After a point, the lift is practiced in its entirety. Remedial exercises play a part of the program.

Practice Layouts by Class

Chart 11 outlines the number of times the grouped categories are practiced each week, for each class and the time allotted per workout for the exercises. Technique exercises are at the beginning of practices.

Elite

	Day #1	Day #2	Day #3	Day #4	Day #5
a.m.	1. Sn Tech	1. C&J Tech	1. Jk Tech	1. C&J Tech	1. Leg
	2. Sn Pw	2. Cl Pw	2. Cl Pw	2. Sn Tech	2. Jk Pw
	3. Jk Pw	3. Jk Pw	3. Jk Pw	3. Jk Pw	3. Sn Pw
	4. Jk Tech	4. Sn Tech	4. Leg	4. Cl Pw	4. Cl Tech
p.m.	5. Sn Pw	5. Sn Pw	5. Sn Pw	5. Leg	5. Jk Pw
	6. Leg	6. Cl Pw	6. Shlder Remed	6. Leg Remed	6. Cl Pw
	7. Shldr Remed	7. Leg Remed	7. Bk Remed	7. Bk Remed	7. Leg

Exercise	Time Allotted (minutes)		
	Prep	Contest	Readaptability
1. Snatch Tech, Clean & Jerk Tech	35	30	20
2. Snatch Power, Clean Power	20-25	20-25	15
3. Jerk Tech & Power, Clean Tech	20	15	5-7
4. Leg	25-30	20-25	15
5. Remedials	15	10	10
6. Warm ups	15	15	10
7. Games	40	20	25
Approximate Total Hours	3	2.25	1.5-1.75

Master

	Day #1	Day #2	Day #3	Day #4	Day #5
a.m.	1. Sn Tech	1. C&J Tech	1. Jk Tech	1. C&J Tech	1. Leg
	2. Sn Pw	2. Cl Pw	2. Jk Pw	2. Sn Tech	2. Jk Pw
	3. Jk Pw	3. Jk Pw	3. Sn Pw	3. Jk Pw	3. Sn Pw
p.m.	4. Jk Tech	4. Sn Tech	4. Leg	4. Cl Pw	4. Cl Tech
	5. Leg	5. Sn Pw	5. Shlder Remed	5. Leg	6. Cl Pw
	6. Bk Remed	6. Cl Pw	6. Bk Remed	6. Leg Remed	7. Shldr Rem
		7. Leg Remed			

Exercise	Time Allotted (minutes)		
	Prep	Contest	Readaptability
1. Snatch Tech, Clean & Jerk Tech	30-35	25-30	15-20
2. Snatch Power, Clean Power	20-25	20-25	15
3. Jerk Tech & Power, Clean Tech	15	15	5
4. Leg	20-25	15-20	15
5. Remedials	10	10	5-7
6. Warm ups	15	15	10
7. Games	40	20	20
Approximate Total Hours	2.5-2.75	2-2.25	1.5

Class I

Day #1	Day #2	Day #3	Day #4	Day #5
1. Sn Tech	1. C&J Tech	1. Jk Tech	1. C&J Tech	1. Cl Tech
2. Sn Pw	2. Sn Tech	2. Jk Pw	2. Sn Tech	2. Leg
3. Jk Tech	3. Cl Pw	3. Cl Pw	3. Jk Pw	3. Jk Pw
4. Leg	4. Jk Pw	4. Leg	4. Cl Pw	4. Sn Pw
5. Bk Remed	5. Leg Remed	5. Shlder Remed	5. Leg Remed	5. Cl Pw
		6. Bk Remed		6. Shldr Remed

Exercise	Time Allotted (minutes)		
	Prep	Contest	Readaptability
1. Snatch Tech, Clean & Jerk Tech	25-30	20-25	15
2. Snatch Power, Clean Power	20	20	12
3. Jerk Tech & Power, Clean Tech	15	15	5
4. Leg	20	15	12
5. Remedials	10	10	5-7
6. Warm ups	15	15	10
7. Games	30	15	15
Approximate Total Hours	2.25	1.75	1.25

Chart 11. Exercises by class (continued on next page)

Class II

Day #1	Day #2	Day #3	Day #4	Day #5
1. Sn Tech	1. C&J Tech	1. Jk Tech	1. C&J Tech	1. Cl Tech
2. Sn Pw	2. Cl Pw	2. Leg	2. Sn Tech	2. Jk Pw
3. Jk Tech	3. Jk Pw	3. Shldr Remed	3. Jk Pw	3. Leg
4. Jk Tech (?)	4. Leg Remed	4. Bk Remed	4. Cl Pw	4. Sn Pw
5. Bk Remed			5. Leg Remed	5. Shldr Remed

Time Allotted (minutes)

Exercise	Prep	Contest	Readaptability
1. Snatch Tech, Clean & Jerk Tech	20-25	20	12
2. Snatch Power, Clean Power	15	15	10
3. Jerk Tech & Power, Clean Tech	15	10	5
4. Leg	15	12-15	10
5. Remedials	10	10	5-7
6. Warm ups	10	10	10
7. Games	25	15	15
Approximate Total Hours	1.75	1.25	1-1.25

Class III

Day #1	Day #2	Day #3	Day #4	Day #5
1. Sn Tech	1. C&J Tech	1. Jk Tech	1. C&J Tech	
2. Cl Tech	2. Jk Pw	2. Sn Tech	2. Jk Pw	
3. Cl Pw	3. Sn Pw	3. Cl Pw	3. Sn Pw	
4. Leg	4. Leg Remed	4. Leg	4. Bk Remed	
5. Shldr Remed	5. Bk Remed	5. Shldr Remed		

Time Allotted (minutes)

Exercise	Prep	Contest	Readaptability
1. Snatch Tech, Clean & Jerk Tech	15-20	15	10
2. Snatch Power, Clean Power	12-15	12	8
3. Jerk Tech & Power, Clean Tech	10	10	5
4. Leg	12-15	12	8
5. Remedials	10	10	5
6. Warm ups	10	10	10
7. Games	20	15	10
Approximate Total Hours	1.5-1.75	1.5	1

Class IV

Day #1	Day #2	Day #3
1. Sn Tech	1. C&J Tech	1. C&J Tech
2. Cl Tech	2. Cl Pw	2. Sn Tech
3. Jk Pw	3. Jk Tech	3. Sn Pw
4. Leg	4. Jk Pw	4. Leg
5. Bk Remed	5. Leg Remed	5. Shldr Remed

Time Allotted (minutes)

Exercise	Prep	Contest	Readaptability
1. Snatch Tech, Clean & Jerk Tech	15	15	5
2. Snatch Power, Clean Power	12-15	12	5
3. Jerk Tech & Power, Clean Tech	10	10	5
4. Leg	12-15	10	5
5. Remedials	5	5	5
6. Warm ups	10	10	10
7. Games	15	10	10
Approximate Total Hours	1.25-1.5	1.25	0.75

Games

Games are used in the workout schedule for good reasons. One is to increase cardiovascular capacity, which contributes to endurance. Anyone claiming that weightlifting is not an endurance effort does not understand the sport. Substantial endurance is required to remain energized for the many hours of competition at a meet. Better-than-adequate cardiovascular capacity will help your lifting enormously.

Another good reason to engage in games is to reinforce movement patterns that are similar to those used in weightlifting. This is why, for example, volleyball and basketball are good choices. If you have ever played a good game of either one, you know how much your legs and hips get worked. The long jump, high jump and shot put are valuable complements because the power movements are similar to lifting. By the way, have you tried ski jumping?

Notes

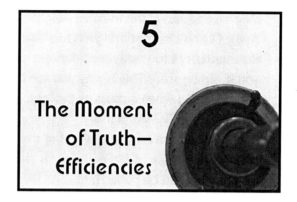

5

The Moment of Truth— Efficiencies

Superior speed is one of the more important athletic qualities required to become a top lifter. This refers to the speed applied to the bar when pulling or jerking, and it also applies to the speed of pulling or pushing one's body under the bar.

Some people think that the hardest skill to master in Olympic-style weightlifting is raising the bar off the floor. I believe it is even harder to master the final pull *under* the bar. Most lifters pull the bar or push the bar with equal power, but efficiency in getting under the bar can separate first place from tenth place.

When executing this *catch* movement of the lift, many athletes rely on the speed of the upward moving bar and simply drop under it. Newton's third law of physics states that for every action there is an equal and opposite reaction. If you pull or push yourself under the bar, you will get under the bar faster than if you just drop below it. By applying continuous force on the bar, it will come to rest in the exact correct position, either overhead in the snatch, or cradled across the chest in the clean.

Now, of course, even if you know what to do, it is another thing to do it. Pulling oneself under a heavily weighted bar requires an absolute commitment to the lift. I have heard foreign coaches call this courage. It takes courage to get under a heavily weighted bar. This is where that heavy chunk of metal and rubber can come crashing down on you, or so it seems. It is like the horns of a bull grazing the matador in the pass.

Courage differs by sport. For some sports it is very evident, like the head-on tackle in football, or rebounding under the basket against massive defenders, in basketball. For some other sports, courage is more subtle, like throwing the legs high above the bar in the pole vault, a somersault over the balance beam, or a tight spin in ice skating.

Although it takes courage to get yourself under a heavily loaded bar, and you may have flashes of this massive weight crashing on you, crashes rarely occur, which is why Olympic weightlifting has the lowest injury rate in the summer Olympics. (For that matter, not too many matadors get gored either!) The illusion feels real, though, and it can be scary. This is why you see lifters back away from the bar. If the bar is not controlled when it starts its descent, it can drop very suddenly. With this lack of control, a lifter can get skittish.

When the athlete is afraid of the bar, he or she may pull the bar too high in order to get under it. Film analysis shows this. The lifter will only succeed with weights that can be pulled high, and this becomes limiting. Weights will be lighter than what the lifter is truly capable of lifting. Efficient lifters pull maximal weights just high enough to barely push or pull themselves beneath. A more timid athlete may pull with great power, but miss the lift because the bar is pulled too high, wasting precious strength and energy.

Is courage innate or can it be learned? It sure helps if it is innate, but I have seen time and again that it can be learned. To do it, break down the lift and find the precise moment in the lift when you want to pull or push yourself under the bar. Practice with light weight, and imagine the situation, trying to bring up the actual emotional response. Practice it over and over again until you overcome your fear, and then go out on the competitive platform and do it.

Three exercises, or efficiencies, that I have found to be very valuable are described below. They help train lifters to pull or push themselves under the bar and not just drop beneath it. Do 4 to 5 repetitions of each at the start of your workout.

Snatch Efficiencies

Begin with the weighted bar on stands or a power rack. Raise the bar to around chest height as you rise up onto the balls of the feet. This is the position at the top of the pull. Lean back slightly. Your elbows are deeply bent and your knees are slightly bent. Hold this position briefly and then perform the snatch by pulling under the bar into a squat. Do 4 to 5 repetitions with light weight. This can be a very successful method for learning to pull, and push, oneself under the bar. If you cannot assume the starting position described, then the weight is too heavy. This is a very poor leverage position so practice with light weight. Start with a broomstick or an unweighted bar.

Clean Efficiencies

As in the snatch efficiencies, use stands in this exercise. While balancing on the balls of your feet, lean back slightly and raise the bar to around belly-button height. Your knees will be slightly bent. Hold this position briefly, then pull yourself quickly under the bar and into a squat. This is a stronger leverage position than in the snatch efficiency but it is still best to use a light weight. Practice 4 to 5 repetitions.

Jerk Efficiencies

Beginning in a semi-split position, raise and hold the bar at hairline height. Quickly jerk the bar by straightening your arms and pushing into a deeper split beneath it, moving your feet to do so. You will not be able to use much weight in this exercise, either, because you're limited by the start position. You will probably use less weight than in the clean efficiencies. Do 4 to 5 repetitions.

Notes

6

Training for Effective Speed and Strength

This chapter has two parts. In the first, I address the importance of speed, and in the second part, I address the importance of strength.

There are a lot of strong lifters in the world, but very few high caliber Olympic lifters. This is because Olympic weightlifting is a subtle blend of speed and strength, the combination of which translates to power. It is not sufficient to be very strong. Neither is it enough to be quick. One must develop the correct balance of each to maximize lifting potential.

To become a top Olympic lifter, you must have speed. I am talking about speed pulling or jerking the bar, and speed pulling or pushing oneself under the bar. Watch highly ranked lifters and observe how fast they are. Dr. Tamas Ajan, President of the International Weightlifting Federation, once told me that American lifters are, in general, slower than the European lifters. American lifters also rank lower than their European counterparts internationally. This is not a coincidence.

Why is this? I was curious, too. After years of informal interviews and study, it was clear to me that the American athletes had become slow by working almost exclusively with heavy weights on assistance exercises, like pulls and squats. As a result, they developed strength at the expense of speed. While heavy lifting gave them demonstrably greater strength in those exercises, it was a type of strength that inhibited speed in the Olympic lifts. Without sufficient speed work, their snatches and clean and jerks became sluggish.

Many factors influence an athlete's speed. Naturally, structural aspects of an athlete's physiology, such as leverage and muscle quality, affect lifting performance, but so does the right kind of training. Speed is a function of the right kind of hard work. It behooves a lifter to develop *effective speed*, because without it, one will get stuck in a weight range below their actual capability.

Let me explain what I mean by *effective speed*. In his book, *Scientific Principles of Coaching*, John Bunn shows that with maximum strength, you have no speed, and conversely, with maximum speed, you have no strength. He demonstrates that the most effective speed is one-half the maximum speed, and the most effective strength is one-half the maximum strength. A weightlifter cannot be effective using near maximum strength or near maximum speed because maximum lifts depend on the right combination of both. On a perfect day, a lifter can break personal records with ease. Might such a day be the result of the perfect balance of speed and strength?

If effective speed and effective strength are one-half the maximum of each, then to raise one's lifting totals, it makes sense to raise maximums. One-half a higher maximum is better than one-half a lower maximum. Acquiring maximum speed means training the fast-twitch muscle fibers within the ranges of motion that most count, near the four most effective leverage positions. These positions include the start position when the bar is on the floor, when the bar is just off the floor, when it is just above the knee and then when it is two thirds the way up the thigh.

I developed exercises to maximize effective speed with the following in mind:

- Fast-twitch muscle fibers can go all out for only 5 to 12 seconds, with the average range between 6 to 8 seconds.
- Fast-twitch muscle fibers need a minimum of 45 seconds and a maximum of 4 minutes, to recuperate.
- The entire program must be practical relative to the time allocated to the total program. If more bouts and more rest and more days would accomplish more in relationship to the total program, I would propose more.
- In training for maximum speed, use very light weights.
- It is difficult to train for effective speed throughout the whole range of motion because with little or no weight, the snatch and clean and jerk become ballistic motions. The bone outruns the muscle and the coordination occurs around the most effective bone leverage positions. This does not train the muscles to respond quickly with heavy weights.
- In training for maximum speed, the tendency is to cut short the movements at the top—therefore, catch the weight with straight knees when possible. This requires the athlete to perform the full movement.

Speed Training Component

The speed program follows. Practice this program at the beginning of the competition season, for six to eight weeks. Do this program at least twice a week, but no more than three times a week. More than this will cut into the time required to complete the total program and will diminish the benefits of both. How much weight should you use for these exercises? Work light. If you need to bend your knees to catch the bar, the weight is too high.

1. Stretch—alternate cardiovascular work and stretching exercises for 20 minutes.

2. Power Snatch from the Knee—begin the power snatch just above the knee and catch the bar with straight knees. Move as fast as possible, but be sure to set before each repetition. Do 3 to 6 sets of 10 to 14 repetitions; rest 45 seconds between each set.

3. Push Jerk from the Shoulder—jerk from the shoulder and catch it with straight knees. Go as fast as possible, but set before each repetition. Do 3 to 6 sets of 10 to14 repetitions; rest 45 to 60 seconds between each set. Note that after driving the bar, you must slow it down at the top to avoid hyperextending the elbows. Later, you may fully extend the elbow, but only after you have developed maximum strength in the throw from the shoulder.

4. Clean Pull from above Knee—perform the pull from just above the knee. Do not whip the bar over because this is something else (important, but different). Pull the bar to just under your sternum. Pull as fast as possible, and set before each repetition. Do 3 to 6 sets of 10 to 14 repetitions; rest 1 minute between each set.

5. Choose one of the following:

5a. Run Down a Slight Grade—find a slope about 35 to 50 yards long with a grade steep enough to get your legs moving faster than you normally run, but not so steep that you use your legs to brake yourself. Run the grade 12 to 15 times, resting 1 minute between each run.

5b. Run 35 to 50 yard sprints—run 12 to15 times and rest 1 minute between each run.

5c. (Use some common sense on this one!) Run while Hanging onto Device Attached to Car—use a rope or device designed for this purpose and attach it to a car. Run 70 to 90 yards, 12-15 times, resting 1.5 minutes between each run. The car should pull you fast enough so that your legs move faster than you normally run, but not so fast that you will be pulled off balance and fall.

As you can see, this is a demanding workout. It will take time. You should treat it as a separate workout and not as a warm up. Treat it with the same seriousness as your weight-training workout. When doing the power snatch, push jerk and clean pull, use a broomstick or an unloaded bar. You must go all out on every repetition, get set properly and extend fully.

Strength Training Component

The exercises and systems presented, so far, in this book are designed to strengthen and condition your body for the sport of Olympic-style weightlifting. By following my guidelines, you cultivate a very dynamic kind of strength, or functional strength, as it is sometimes called. It is strength in motion, and though this is training for the sport of Olympic lifting, the strength you develop with this kind of training transfers readily to all varieties of athletics and daily activities. This is why the Olympic lifts are used for cross training by so many professional athletic teams.

The strength training component of my program works differently. It is done, in part, with deep penetrating exercise or functional isometrics. Isometric exercise, also known as static strength training, is characterized by two things. First, there is no visible motion in the adjacent joint, and second, the working muscles do not change in length. Isometric exercise is believed to penetrate deeply into the muscle fiber and has been shown to activate more muscle fiber than traditional resistance exercise. What follows is a discussion of some functional isometric exercises that are very effective for developing static strength

A word of caution: this should only be done 1 to 2 times a week. More frequent practice will not result in more progress and can interfere with your other training work. It can be done at anytime during the conditioning phase of your cycle, except for the last.

The exercise I describe here is practiced using a squat or power rack and can be used with clean and snatch pulls, or squats. Use 80 to 130 percent of your maximum weight capacity. The racks must have holes for pegs spaced every 3 to 5 inches. You will need four pegs. Set two pegs, one on each side of the rack, in the corresponding holes. Then set the other two pegs, one on each side of the rack, in the holes just above the first pegs. The pegs should be spaced three to five inches apart. Rest the weighted bar on the lower pegs, set your back and hips, then raise the bar and pull it against the upper pegs. Hold for 3 seconds, and do a total of 3 repetitions.

To maximize the value of this exercise, choose positions you wish to strengthen at separate points within the whole range of motion. To illustrate, choose 3 positions within the full front squat motion. You might select the usual sticking points. The first might be the very bottom of the squat where the hips are in their lowest position. The second might be one where the hips are just below knee height and the third might be the position where the hips are level with the knees.

Set the pegs on the rack at the proper position to work the first sticking point, where the hips are in the lowest position. Rest the weighted bar on the lower pegs. Assume your squat position, with the bar resting across the *shelf*, across your chest at approximately shoulder level and supported by your hands. Elbows are lifted as in the jerk start position. Raise the bar off the lower peg by rising out of the squat and press it against the upper peg. All the effort in this movement is concentrated in the legs. Hold the position for 3 seconds and repeat for a total of 3 reps.

Try this in each of the sticking positions, hips below the knees, at knee height and slightly higher than the knees. Hold it for 3 seconds, 3 reps. If it is easy, add weight. If you can't hold it for 3 reps of 3 seconds, then decrease the weight.

This is also an excellent exercise for developing strength in the pull. When practicing this method with the pull, be sure to maintain a very strong position in the lower back. Brace your back with strong abdominal tension and, as always in Olympic lifting, lift with the legs.

A Word about the Valsalva Maneuver

This is a good time to mention the Valsalva Maneuver and its role in weightlifting. When lifting a heavy weight, it is almost reflexive to take a breath and hold it briefly, or for the duration of the exertion. There is a reason for this. By holding the breath and bracing the torso with it, one is actually creating support for the spine and mid-section. Opinions differ about the affects of this on blood pressure. Some evidence suggests that it will stabilize blood pressure; other evidence suggests that it poses risks.

If you have any concerns about the safety of such lifting, talk it over with your doctor.

Notes

7

Eccentric Contraction— Loading and Deloading, Tetany

Similar to the exercises recommended in the Strength Training Component above, the exercises I describe in this chapter develop a different kind of strength. Keep in mind, though, that this is not functional strength training. This strength does not translate directly into the dynamic movements of Olympic lifting. The exercises in this chapter can help develop strength at very specific points within the lifts' ranges of motion. They can augment your other training but cannot substitute for practicing the lifts themselves. If you are weak coming out of a deep squat, for example, these exercises can help to develop strength in that tiny range where you may have weakness.

Deep Penetrating Exercises

These penetrating exercises work deep into the muscle, reaching into all the muscle's fibers. They have been shown to activate more muscle fiber than traditional progressive resistance exercises and are extremely effective in developing static strength.

You will know you are working deeply into the muscle fiber when you feel your muscles tremble with the effort. The Russians have a term for this. They call it "tetany." Tetany occurs when a muscle's strength is so challenged that tension within the working muscle causes it to shake.

This program of tetany, however, should only be practiced after at least 1 year of training. It takes 1 year, minimum, for tendons and ligaments to develop the strength to safely tolerate the stress of tetany.

What follows are two kinds of exercises that fall into this category of deep penetrating exercises. They are called eccentric and isometric exercise, and both will induce "tetany."

Eccentrics

Most traditional weight training exercises involve *lifting* weight. Lifting or raising weight typically entails a concentric muscle contraction. A dumbbell curl illustrates this clearly. As the dumbbell is raised to shoulder level, the bicep contracts or becomes shortened. Eccentric exercise is the reverse. It involves lowering a weight, slowly and in a very controlled manner. In the example of a reverse bicep curl, the bicep is now trying to lower, and lift, the weight, simultaneously. By lowering the weight very slowly, the muscle has to work to counter the downward pull of the weight, so the effect on the muscle is the same as if it were lifting the weight at the same time it is lowering the weight. This is why eccentrics are such effective strengthening methods in your workouts, and they can be practiced especially successfully using squats or pulls.

But wait! Before you start loading the bar for your eccentrics, find a couple of reliable training partners, because you cannot train at this level of effort without them.

Here is how it works. For an eccentric squat, bend the knees and lower the hips very slowly, taking about six seconds, into the full squat position. The objective is to use more and more weight without losing your form, but here's the kicker. Eccentric exercises are done with 100 – 130 percent of your maximum, i.e., you're beginning with maximal weight, and then you add more in subsequent squats. Once you are at the bottom of your squat, your training partners quickly and simultaneously remove some of the weight from each side of the bar so you can come out of your squat unassisted.

Another excellent eccentric is the snatch pull, which is approached differently than the eccentric squat. If a lifter's best snatch pull is 100 kilos, the lifter will begin with a snatch pull 80 percent of the best, or 80 kilos. When the pull reaches its maximum height, the lifter holds the bar at that height, and the training partners add 10 kilos to each side of the bar. The lifter performs the eccentric contraction by lowering the bar slowly to the floor, taking roughly 4-6 seconds to do so. Once the bar is on the floor, remove the 10s from each end of the bar, and repeat the process 2-3 times.

It is extremely important for the training partners to add the weights at precisely the same time. If one end of the bar is heavier, the lifter may not be able to maintain control of the bar. If the bar tilts abruptly, it can cause a serious injury.

Do the snatch pulls, clean pulls, and squat eccentrics 1-2 times a week during the preparation phase. Incorporating more eccentrics in your workouts will not lead to greater progress.

Eccentric Contraction—Tetany

Eccentric contraction with tetany is a variation of eccentric contraction. Instead of covering the entire range of motion slowly, the lifter lowers the weight and pauses for 2 seconds at 3-5 different positions within the range of motion. Just like the eccentric contraction exercises, eccentric contraction with tetany can be practiced with the squat, snatch pull, and clean pull. The weight criteria are high, 110 – 130 percent of your maximum. You should do 2-3 sets, once a week.

Because this work requires such large weights, you need the help of spotters. As in the example above, when performed with the squat, you will need assistance getting up from the full position. This is very intense training.

If tetany is not induced with this practice, use more weight. If the lifter can't hold the 3-5 positions for 2 seconds each, then reduce the weight. Understand that finding the correct weight for this exercise will be a process.

After practicing eccentric exercise you will find that your muscles now have considerable stored energy. When you are done, try pulling or squatting as forcefully as possible to use this stored energy to your advantage.

Notes

8

Intensity Programs

Over training is a common mistake made by many weight training beginners. Even very experienced lifters think the only good training session is one where they go all out, every time. They do not feel satisfied if they donít lift heavy.

This is limiting because it is impossible to work at maximal capacity and make progress with every workout. After a few months, progress becomes more and more elusive. It is sad to see people make this mistake. They train really hard, make progress for a few months and then they plateau. So they work even harder with still no progress and finally they grow discouraged and quit. They blame themselves for failure. Remember Selye.

A lack of progress leads to frustration and discouragement. Injuries can occur, and even illness. This is not imaginary. Real changes take place when the body is constantly blasted. Adrenaline and cortisols are depleted and eosinophil levels go way up, a sure sign that the body is over stressed. This happens because the athlete is playing in the Super Bowl, the NBA finals *and* the World Series in every workout.

Because weight training is easily measured, lifters have a tendency to test and measure themselves all the time. Almost all athletes whose sports can be measured in time, distance or weight have the same tendency. This is competitive psychology. In the absence of a rival, one competes against oneself, which can lead to over training.

Professional athletes don't go all out at every practice. They train continuously but change their workouts. When not peaking, they work to lay the groundwork for future progress. Then when they do go all out, they are prepared to do their best.

In the perfect world, every workout would improve the athlete, and the athlete would have fun doing it. There is a joy to lifting, throwing and jumping smoothly. To lift a heavy bar effortlessly is pleasing, and that is why we do it. But also give yourself the freedom to work with different, and especially, lighter weights. This will allow you to walk away from a workout, feeling refreshed physically and mentally. It is a super feeling!

Over the years I have developed many intensity guidelines to help you train sensibly by balancing heavy training with periods of rest. The intensity guidelines can be used for complete motions of the Olympic lifts, partial motions, and pulls. They also can be applied to bench presses, pullovers, squats, dead lifts, and hip and leg barbell curls. These are guidelines. Be flexible with them, and make adjustments when necessary.

Some lifters choose not to practice the Olympic lifts to gain strength and muscle, and there is some logic to this. Since the Olympic lifts are so athletically demanding, technique can fail after several repetitions. This could lead to injury or at the very least, exhaustion, before strength gain is achieved. Shortening the range of motion is one solution to this. Break the lifts into their component motions, and you can practice elements of the Olympic lifts to develop strength.

For the Olympic lifter, there is nothing that can match the muscle developed by practicing the shortened ranges of motion of the lifts at high repetitions (8 to 12 reps). Because the resulting cardiovascular effort is so great, the athlete also gains a huge caloric burn and an efficient cardiovascular system. All this, and muscle, too!

High numbers of repetitions develop strength and are especially successful when applied to specific segments of the Olympic lifts, such as cleans or snatches from the thigh, clean or snatch dead lifts, and pulls or jerks from the rack. It is imperative to practice these motions. This results in maximum transfer of strength and skill. Time and opportunity are lost rehearsing motions that do not support the two Olympic lifts. Practice technique and build strength at the same time.

In these intensity programs, warm up with 3 to 4 repetitions for 3 to 4 sets. Start at a light weight and slow to moderate speed. Intensities vary weekly. Adjust the program according to how you feel—flexibility is encouraged.

After you've peaked, attempt a maximum of 1 or 2 repetitions in the final week. If the repetitions are higher than last week's, then peak for the number of repetitions called for, or some number higher than 3.

You will see that in most of these intensity programs, you conclude with one effort at maximum weight. Be aware that sometimes, it is fine not to do the one repetition at maximum weight. In fact, if you are preparing for a competition some weeks away, you may not want to attempt a maximum effort. It may not be practical, or even safe, to perform a maximum for one repetition. Chart 12 shows percentage and repetition equivalents of that one repetition maximum attempt. These are approximations. For example, if you can complete four repetitions at 90 percent of your maximum, you will likely succeed at one attempt of your maximum.

It is not perfect but it works very well. This approach saves needless effort and takes into account the larger objectives of your training program.

Percentage / Repetitions						
100/1	95/2	92.5/3	90/4	87.5/5	85/6	82.5/7
80/8	77.5/9	75/10	72.5/11	70/12	67.5/13	65/14
62.5/15	60/16	57.5/17	55/18	52.5/19	50/20	

Chart 12 . Equalizing Intensity between Various Repetitions (kilos or pounds)

The light-hearted names of the following programs are based on the country or person that inspired the idea (Chart 13a-13i). Percentages are based on empirical data from tens of thousands of lifters from various countries, and all the programs have been adapted for American lifters. Warm-up as usual when using these programs; however, note that in some of the programs, the warm-up is built in. Use high repetition programs only for a short time when practicing shortened ranges of motion, and they are best when used early in the season.

We find this a good way to introduce people to peaking intensities that are short, uncomplicated, and have an easily visible course of action. We also find them fun because they offer a variety of reps to peak from. * = percentage of maximum

Twos (2) – 95%

	sets	reps	%
Week 1			
Day 1	4 x	2	80
Day 2	3 x	2	85
Day 3	4 x	2	80
Week 2			
Day 1	4 x	3	80
Day 2	3 x	3	85
Day 3	4 x	2	80
Week 3			
Day 1	4 x	3	90
Day 2	3 x	2	80
Day 3	2 x	2	95*

Sixes (6) – 85%

	sets	reps	%
Week 1			
Day 1	4 x	3	75
Day 2	4 x	2	80
Day 3	4 x	3	80
Week 2			
Day 1	4 x	4	75
Day 2	4 x	2	80
Day 3	3 x	4	80
Week 3			
Day 1	3 x	3	85
Day 2	4 x	2	80
Day 3	2 x	6	85*

Tens (10) – 75%

	sets	reps	%
Week 1			
Day 1	3 x	5	65
Day 2	4 x	4	70
Day 3	3 x	5	70
Week 2			
Day 1	3 x	6	65
Day 2	3 x	5	70
Day 3	2 x	7	70
Week 3			
Day 1	3 x	6	75
Day 2	4 x	4	70
Day 3	1 x	10	75*

Fours (4) – 90%

	sets	reps	%
Week 1			
Day 1	4 x	2	80
Day 2	4 x	3	80
Day 3	4 x	2	80
Week 2			
Day 1	3 x	4	80
Day 2	4 x	2	80
Day 3	4 x	3	85
Week 3			
Day 1	4 x	3	80
Day 2	3 x	2	85
Day 3	2 x	4	90*

Eights (8) – 80%

	sets	reps	%
Week 1			
Day 1	4 x	4	70
Day 2	4 x	3	75
Day 3	4 x	4	75
Week 2			
Day 1	4 x	5	70
Day 2	3 x	4	75
Day 3	3 x	6	75
Week 3			
Day 1	3 x	5	80
Day 2	8 x	3	75
Day 3	1 x	8	80*

Twelves (12) – 70%

	sets	reps	%
Week 1			
Day 1	3 x	6	60
Day 2	4 x	5	65
Day 3	3 x	6	65
Week 2			
Day 1	3 x	7	60
Day 2	3 x	6	65
Day 3	2 x	9	65
Week 3			
Day 1	2 x	7	70
Day 2	3 x	5	65
Day 3	1 x	12	70*

Chart 13a. Cubanito Peaking for Repetitions

This is very good for a person who doesn't have a lot of time and wants variety.

	Lift #		Sets (Circuits)	Reps	Percentage
Week 1					
Day 1	1		4	3	75
Day 2	2		3	2	80
Day 3	1		3	4	75
Week 2					
Day 1	2		3	3	80
Day 2	1		3	3	77
Day 3	2		3	2	85
		or	2	2	87
Week 3					
Day 1	1		3	3	82
Day 2	2		3	3	80
Day 3	1		3	2	85
		or	2	2	87
Week 4					
Day 1	2		2	3	87
		or	3	4	85
Day 2	1		3	4	77
Day 3	2		3	2	90
Week 5					
Day 1	1		2	3	87
		or	3	4	85
Day 2	2		3	4	80
Day 3	1		2	2	90
Week 6					
Day 1	1		2-3	3	85-87
		or	2	2	90
Day 2	1		2	2	85
Day 3	2		2-3	2	92
		or	2	2	95

Chart 13b. Cubanito for Two Similar Motions

This is a solid way to achieve a peak for 1 repetition.

	Percentage	Reps		Percentage	Reps
Week 1			**Week 4**		
Day 1	55	5	Day 1	57	5
	62	4		65	4
	70	3		72	3
	75	2		80	1
				87	2
Day 2	55	5			
	62	4	Day 2	57	5
	70	3		65	4
	77	5		72	3
				80	2
Day 3	55	5			
	62	4	Day 3	57	5
	70	3		62	4
	75	2		72	3
	80	4		80	2
Week 2			**Week 5**		
Day 1	57	5	Day 1	60	5
	65	4		67	4
	72	3		75	3
	80	5		82	2
				87	3
Day 2	57	5			
	65	4	Day 2	60	5
	72	3		67	4
	77	2		75	3
	82	3		82	1
				90	2
Day 3	57	5			
	65	4	Day 3	60	5
	72	3		67	4
	80	6		75	3
				80	4
Week 3					
Day 1	57	5	**Week 6**		
	65	4	Day 1	60	4
	72	3		67	3
	77	6		75	2
				80	2
Day 2	57	5			
	65	4	Day 2	60	4
	72	3		67	3
	77	2		75	2
	85	3		82	4
Day 3	57	5	Day 3	60	3
	65	4		67	3
	72	3		75	2
	80	6		82	1-2
				87	1
				92	2x2
				or	
				95	3x1

Chart 13c. Hungarian—as Blue as the Danube

This is another program of relatively short duration—4 weeks. It has the advantage of the Cubanitos. These are valuable if you need something of short duration. * = percentage of maximum

Latin Mescal #1

	Sets (Circuits)	Reps	%
Week 1			
Day 1	1	4	70
	2	3	80
	1	3	75
Day 2	1	3	70
	2	2	85
	1	3	80
Day 3	1	3	70
	2	3	80
	1	4	75
Week 2			
Day 1	1	4	70
	2	4	80
	1	4	75
Day 2	1	4	70
	1	2	80
	1	3	85
Day 3	1	3	70
	2	3	85
	1	4	80
Week 3			
Day 1	1	3	70
	1	3	80
	2	2	90
	1	4	80
Day 2	1	4	70
	1	2	80
	2	3	85
Day 3	1	3	70
	1	6	85*
	1	6	80*
Week 4			
Day 1	1	3	70
	1	2	80
	2	4	90*
Day 2	Rest		
Day 3	1	3	70
	1	2	80
	1	2	95*
	1	2	90*

Latin Mescal #2

	Sets (Circuits)	Reps	%
Week 1			
Day 1	1	4	70
	1	2	80
	2	3	75
	1	5	70
Day 2	1	3	70
	2	3	80
	1	4	75
Day 3	1	4	70
	1	3	80
	2	4	75
Week 2			
Day 1	1	5	70
	3	4	80
Day 2	1	3	70
	1	2	80
	2	4	75
Day 3	1	4	70
	1	3	80
	2	6	75
Week 3			
Day 1	1	3	70
	2	3	85
	2	5	80
Day 2	1	4	70
	2	2	85
	1	3	75
Day 3	1	4	70
	1-2	8	80*
Week 4			
Day 1	1	3	70
	1	3	80
	1	6	85*
	1	6	80*
Day 2	Rest		
Day 3	1	2	70
	1	2	80
	2	4	90*

Chart 13d. Latin Mescal #1 & #2

	Circuits (sets)	Reps	%		Circuits (sets)	Reps	%
Week 1				**Week 5**			
Day 1	1	2-4	50	Day 1	1	2-4	55
	1	2-4	60		1	2-4	65
	5	5	70		4	5	75
Day 2	1	2-4	55	Day 2	1	2-4	55
	1	2-4	65		1	2-4	65
	4-5	4	75		1	2	75
					2	3	85
Day 3	1	2-4	50				
	1	2-4	60	Day 3	1	2-4	60
	1	2	70		1	2-3	70
	3-4	4	80		1	2	80
					1	1	87
Week 2					1-2	2	92
Day 1	1	2-4	55				
	1	2-4	65	**Week 6**			
	4-5	5	75	Day 1	1	2-4	55
					1	2-4	65
Day 2	1	2-4	50		5	5	75
	1	2-4	60				
	1	2	70	Day 2	1	2-4	60
	3-4	4-5	80		1	2-4	65
					1	2	75
Day 3	1	2-4	55		3	4	85
	1	2-4	65				
	1	2	75	Day 3	1	2-4	60
	2-3	3-4	85		1	2-3	70
					1	2	80
Week 3					1	1	87
Day 1	1	2-4	50		1	2	95
	1	2-4	60				
	5	5	70				
Day 2	1	2-4	55				
	1	2-4	65				
	1	2	72				
	3	4	80				
Day 3	1	2-4	60				
	1	2-3	70				
	1	2	80				
	2-3	2-3	87				
Week 4							
Day 1	1	2-4	50				
	1	2-4	60				
	5	5	70				
Day 2	1	2-4	55				
	1	2-4	65				
	1	2	72				
	4	5	80				
Day 3	1	2-4	60				
	1	2-3	70				
	2	2	90				

Chart 13e. Methodically English or the Turtle Will Always Get There

This is a well-put-together, inclusive program for peaking for one repetition. One of the sets will be between the percentages when a range is shown.

Day 1	Weeks 1 & 2 %	Weeks 3 & 4 %	Weeks 5 & 6 %
Snatch floor, 4x2	82-85	87-90	95
Snatch pull floor, 2x2	95	102-105	107-112
Snatch thigh, 2x2	85-87	90-92	95-97
Snatch pull thigh, 2x2	100-105	112-115	102-107
Snatch dead lift, 2x2	107-115	117-122	107-112

Day 2	Weeks 1 & 2 %	Weeks 3 & 4 %	Weeks 5 & 6 %
C & J floor, 4x2	82	87	92
C & J pull floor, 2x2	95-100	102-105	105-110
C & J thigh, 2x2	87	87-90	92-95
C & J pull thigh, 2x2	100-102	107-112	102-107
C & J dead lift	105-112	115-120	105-110

This also works for combinations of similar motions of: 1) jerk front and 2) jerk back

Chart 13f. Oriental for Two Similar Motions

This is the best basic, no frills, percentage program.

Week 1

Day 1		Day 2		Day 3	
70%	1x2	70%	1x2	70%	1x2
75%	1x2	75%	1x2	75%	1x2
80%	4x2	80%	4x3	80%	4x2

Week 2

Day 1		Day 2		Day 3	
70%	1x2	70%	1x2	70%	1x2
75%	1x2	75%	1x2	75%	1x2
80%	4x4	80%	4x2	80%	4x5

Week 3

Day 1		Day 2		Day 3	
70%	1x2	70%	1x2	70%	1x2
75%	1x2	75%	1x2	75%	1x2
80%	4x2	80%	4x4	80%	4x2

Week 4

Day 1		Day 2		Day 3	
70%	1x2	70%	1x2	70%	1x2
75%	1x2	75%	1x2	75%	1x2
85%	3x5	80%	4x2	90%	3x4

Week 5

Day 1		Day 2		Day 3	
70%	1x2	70%	1x2	70%	1x2
75%	1x2	75%	1x2	75%	1x2
80%	4x2	90%	2X3	80%	4x2

Week 6

Day 1		Day 2		Day 3	
70%	1x2	70%	1x2	70%	1x2
75%	1x2	75%	1x2	75%	1x2
100%	2x2	80%	4x2	105%	2x1

Chart 13g. Soviet Original

This is especially good for the dead lift, squat and presses. It also can be used with shortened motions such as the power snatch and power clean from the thigh.

	Percentage	Reps		Percentage	Reps
Week 1			**Week 4**		
Day 1	50	10	Day 1	55	10
	65	7		70	6
	80	4		80	2
	70	9		90	2x3
Day 2	50	10	Day 2	55	10
	70	6		65	7
	85	5		80	4
	75	8		65	10
Day 3	50	10	Day 3	55	10
	60	7		70	6
	80	4		80	2
	70	10		90	3x3
Week 2			**Week 5**		
Day 1	55	10	Day 1	55	7
	70	6		65	4
	85	4		80	3
	75	6		70	5
	65	9		70	5
				60	8
Day 2	55	10			
	65	7	Day 2	55	7
	80	4		70	3
	70	9		80	2
	70	9		95	2x2
Day 3	55	10	Day 3	55	7
	70	8		65	4
	85	5		80	3
	65	9		65	8
Week 3			**Week 6**		
Day 1	55	10	Day 1	55	5
	65	7		70	3
	80	4		82	2
	70	9		97	3x3
			Or	100	2x2
Day 2	55	9	Day 2	Rest	
	70	6			
	80	2	Day 3	55	7
	90	2		70	4
	80	6		85	3
				70	6
Day 3	55	10			
	70	7			
	80	4			
	65	10			

Chart 13h. A Bulgarian Peaking Program—The Land of Yogurt

This program combines high reps for gaining muscle (and strength), and low reps for gaining muscle density (strength with little or no size gain). High reps are defined as 5-12 reps, low reps 1-4 reps. High reps work well with partial motions.

High Reps

	Reps	%	Sets
Day 1	10	65	2-3
Day 3	8	75	2
Day 5	6	77	2-3
Day 7	12	65	2
Day 9	10	70	2-3
Day 11	9	72	2
Day 13	8	70	2-3
Day 15	5	82	2-3
Day 17	7	77	2
Day 19	5	80	2-3
Day 21	6	75	2

Low Reps

	Reps	%	Sets
Day 2	4	77	3-4
Day 4	3	80	3
Day 6	2	82	3-4
Day 8	4	80	3
Day 10	3	85	2-4
Day 12	4	82	2-3
Day 14	2	87	2
Day 16	4	80	2-3
Day 18	2	90	3-4
Day 20	3	87	2-3
Day 22	2	92	1-2

Chart 13i. Wild West—High Ball / Low Ball

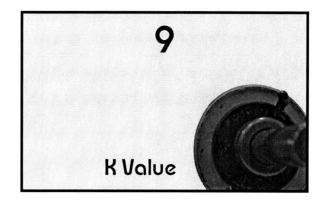

9

K Value

The K value expresses the relationship of intensity to your goal for the total lifted in the two Olympic lifts. It is a useful guideline that will help you determine how intensely to train for a specific total or goal. Let me explain what is involved.

$$K = \frac{Ia \times 100}{Total}$$

In the K-value formula, *Ia* represents your average intensity. To calculate your average intensity, add up the pounds you lift at 70 percent or more of your goal for the next contest. Count all squats, pulls, dead lifts, Olympic lifts, and anything else lifted. Divide the number of pounds lifted by the number of repetitions, and that gives you the average amount of weight you lifted during your workout. In other words, it is the average intensity at which you train.

$$Ia = \frac{Total\ Pounds\ Lifted}{Number\ of\ Repetitions}$$

Let's say you lift 25,500 pounds in 100 repetitions. When you divide 25,500 by 100, your average intensity equals 255 pounds.

$$255 = \frac{25,500}{100}$$

The average intensity is either going to stimulate your body to develop more strength or not. If your average intensity goes up and the total is the same, then the

K value is higher. If your average intensity goes down, and your total remains the same, then the K value drops.

Next, determine how much you wish to lift at the next meet. For example, let's say your goal is a total of 700 pounds. Using the formula, multiply 255 by 100 and divide it by 700. The K value is 36.43.

$$K = \frac{255 \times 100}{700}$$
$$K = 36.43$$

Now let's say that months later you have changed the intensity of your workout but maintained the same goal. You still hope to lift a total of 700 pounds but during *this* training phase, your intensity is just 240 pounds per training session. During this period, average intensity was 15 pounds less than before, when you lifted an average of 255 pounds.

$$K = \frac{240 \times 100}{700}$$
$$K = 34.3$$

Using the formula, the K value equals 240 times 100 divided by 700 for a total of 34.3. Did you make more progress when the K value was 36.43 or when it was 34.3? There is no right answer, only the right answer for you. Did you make more progress lifting at a higher average intensity or lower average intensity? Here lies the value of the K. If you can establish a trend for a certain K value, workouts can be adjusted to always have that K value. A successful K value for your friend may be different from your K value. Some people will perform best at the higher, some at the lower value.

Back to our example…Congratulations! You make the 700 total with a K value of 36.43! We can assume that a K value of 36.43 was a successful ratio of weight lifted to actual number of lifts. It worked for your body to train at that intensity.

(This is a good place to mention that the best progress in the United States is being made with K values between 32 and 38 percent. Higher values are associated with better conditioning. Better conditioning usually results in quicker recovery after high intensity workouts.)

So you made the 700 pound goal. What happens when you want to increase your goal to, say, 730 pounds? Consider working at the same intensity level and keeping the K value constant. You must adjust the average intensity to reach your new total.

Now we go back to the formula and plug in the known values. Keeping K at 36.43, and increasing the total to 730, the average intensity is 266 pounds, or *la* = 266. You can adjust the number of repetitions and poundage so that the average intensity comes out to 266 pounds. You will be applying the same level of intensity to your new, higher goal of 730 pounds.

$$36.43 = \frac{la \times 100}{730}$$

$$la = 266$$

The key to progress is intensity. I cannot stress enough the importance of planning around the K value. It is a basic and simple tool. You will make progress only when you increase intensity, and the amount of that increase can best be discovered through the K value.

Now that we have come this far, let me review and give some other pointers for using the K value. First, when calculating intensity (the amount of pounds divided by repetitions) count squats, pulls, dead lifts, and any other weighted exercises you practice.

Second, in calculating the pounds for intensity, count only repetitions performed at 70 percent or more of your goal for the next contest. Pulls can be included in this group of exercises, but remember that pulls are based on what you want to snatch or clean, not your best snatch pull or clean pull. Count all lifts that are at least 70 percent of your expected snatch and expected clean.

Third, be realistic when you set goals for a meet. Experience will provide the necessary guidelines. A good rule of thumb is that after the lifting season is over, take your best total and subtract seven to ten percent to identify your first goal of the coming season. This will provide psychological rest. Then build from there. By backing off of your best previous performance, you also get physical rest. This is so important. The body cannot respond to unrelenting pressure and stress all year.

Fourth, calculate the K value on a monthly basis. If you are preparing for a contest for which you are peaking, calculate it on a weekly basis from week six though week two in final peaking.

This brings me to a last, but important, point. Condition your heart and vascular strength at a time when there is no pressure to lift at the high end of your range. Run dashes; bicycle; swim; high jump; play soccer, volleyball or basketball on a regular basis. Getting into cardiovascular shape early in your lifting year paves the way to training at your optimum K value as the year progresses. You will find that you recover quicker from those intensity workouts when you're in shape early. Later in the year, a little training will suffice to maintain condition.

Notes

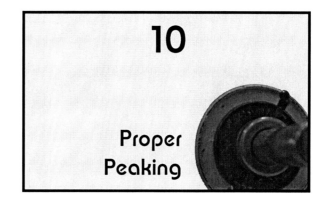

10

Proper Peaking

n preparation for competition, it is important to schedule your training intensities so that you peak at the appropriate time. The following peaking intensities are designed to help you do this. With proper training in the preparation phase and early in the contest phase, you will be ready for the competition. This is done successfully in Europe because they have experience with different peaking intensities two to three weeks before a contest.

It is important to be aware of the variation in peaking intensity among the weight classes. Lifters in the lighter classes can peak closer to the contest, while those in the heavier classes need more time to recuperate from a high peaking intensity. It is more difficult for a heavier-class lifter to develop speed, too. As the contest approaches, a heavier-class lifter can concentrate on training for speed using lighter weights. In fact, these lifters might need speed training even more than lighter-class lifters.

In Chart 14, the classes are grouped by how they respond to different peaking intensities. Accordingly, the 56 and 62 kilo classes are grouped together; the 69, 77 and 85 kilo classes are another group; and the 94 to 105 kilo classes makeup a third group. Finally, the super heavyweights are by themselves. Naturally, there are deviations from this. For women, the classes are similarly grouped. Women in the 48 and 53 kilo classes should follow the guidelines for the men's 56 and 62 kilo group. Women in the 58 and 63 kilo classes use the same strategy as the 69, 77, and 85 kilo men's group. Women lifting in the 69, 75, and 75+ kilo classes should follow the guidelines for the men's 94 to 105 kilo classes. The guidelines for each group are based on overall trends, knowing that a small percentage of lifters will have to be treated individually.

56 – 62 Kilo Classes

Days before contest	Snatch	Clean & Jerk	Snatch Pull	Clean Pull	Leg	Heavy partial movmts	Simulated Jerk movmts	Technique movmts
10-12	100+	100+	110	105	100+	115	100+	100+
8-9	97	95	107	105	100+	110	95	95
6-7	95	90	102	100	90	105	90	90
4-5	90	85	100	95	85	100	85	85
3	85	80	95	90	80			
2	80	75	90	85	75			
1	70	65						

69 – 77 Kilo Classes

Days before contest	Snatch	Clean & Jerk	Snatch Pull	Clean Pull	Leg	Heavy partial movmts	Simulated Jerk movmts	Technique movmts
13-14	100+	100+	110	107	100+	117	100+	100+
11-12	97	95	107	105	100+	112	95	95
9-10	97	95	107	102	97	107	92	95
7-8	95	90	105	100	95	102	90	90
5-6	92	87	100	97	90	97	87	87
4	87	82	97	92	82	92	82	82
3	82	77	92	87	77			
2	77	72	87	82	72			
1	70	65						

85 – 105 Kilo Classes

Days before contest	Snatch	Clean & Jerk	Snatch Pull	Clean Pull	Leg	Heavy partial movmts	Simulated Jerk movmts	Technique movmts
15-17	100+	100+	115	110	100+	120	100+	100+
12-14	97	95	110	105	100+	112	95	95
9-11	95	90	105	100	95	105	90	90
6-8	92	87	100	95	90	100	85	87
4-5	87	85	95	90	85	90	80	85
3	80	75	90	85	77			
2	72	67	82	77	70			
1	65	60						

Over 105 Kilo Classes (Super-heavyweight)

Days before contest	Snatch	Clean & Jerk	Snatch Pull	Clean Pull	Leg	Heavy partial movmts	Simulated Jerk movmts	Technique movmts
15-17	97	95	112	107	100+	117	97	85
12-14	95	92	107	102	97	110	95	92
10-11	92	90	105	100	92	102	90	90
8-9	90	85	102	100	90	95	85	85
6-7	85	82	97	95	87	87	80	82
4-5	82	80	92	90	82			
3	77	75	87	82	75			
2	72	67	82	77	70			
1	65	60						

Chart 14. Peaking Intensity Percentages

The percentages in Chart 14 are suggested peaking intensities. In the snatch and snatch pull, base the percentage on your goal for the next contest. Similarly, in the clean and jerk and the clean pull, base the percentage on what you want to clean.

Leg work percentages are based on your best weights for the prescribed number of repetitions. The jerk is broken down into the following three heavy, partial movements: jerk off the rack, front squat and jerk. The percentage for each jerk movement is based on what you plan to jerk at the next contest.

Once you work up to the peaking intensity for a given motion, devote the rest of the time allocated to that exercise. If the target weight is 80 percent of your goal, or more, do not drop to less than 80 percent. If weights are below 80 percent, stay at the peaking intensity suggested.

One of the big frontiers in Olympic lifting is peaking correctly for a contest. Even the wisest athletes have trouble consistently getting the most out of their bodies. The following guidelines will help you time your peak so you can lift better in your contests.

- Muscles work best when you start low and increase the intensity (weight) over the next two or three sets.
- You must increase the level of intensity to progress.
- When you are increasing intensity, you should not stay at high intensity every workout.

Therefore,

Increase Intensity:

- First set, lift comfortably.
- Second set, increase intensity.
- Third set, increase again.
- If you cannot increase, you started too high.
- If you miss two lifts in a row, lower your weight and try to increase again.
- After having increased to a very high level of intensity, the next workout(s) you can go back down in weight! Then in later workouts, try to go back up.

There will come a time when you cannot increase the intensities, either because your muscles are not physiologically capable of doing it, or you are fighting the increases emotionally. In either case do the following

Decrease Intensity:

- Go down in intensity for one, two, or three workouts.
- Then try to increase the intensities again.

You will gain the most power and endurance both in your external muscles and your internal muscles when you pay attention to the intensity guidelines.

In your training sessions, you will lift until you miss within the time allotted for your class. Try to increase your intensity each time. When you miss two lifts in a row, lower the weight, then try to go back up.

11

Cluster Training

any years ago, Peary and Mabel Rader's *Iron Man Magazine* published a system of training in which lifters did maximum or near maximum presses from racks every minute for an hour. This was a simple form of Cluster Training. The practice has been refined since then, but the underlying principal remains sound.

Cluster Training is another useful method when preparing an athlete for competition. It entails "clustering" lifts, or practicing many repetitions of a complete lift. It fills the gap between overloading partial movements, done throughout the preparation phase, and motor setting, which is done in the last two or three weeks of the contest phase.

Before cluster training was developed, something with missing in training. We knew how to train for increased power in a partial range of motion, and we knew how to train the whole movement. Something more was needed to train the whole movement for power.

The advantage of training partial movements is that great overload for a specific range of motion can take place. This is important because it strengthens your weakest and your strongest muscles. After overloading partial movements, though, it is necessary to overload the whole movement by practicing complete lifts with sufficient intensity. Cluster Training accomplishes this.

Cluster Training allows us to overload the complete movement and challenge the fast-twitch muscle fibers to perform. Much has been written on the subject of fast-twitch and slow-twitch muscle types. In weightlifting, we want to work fast-twitch muscle fibers because they contract or fire more rapidly for quick bursts of strength and speed.

Keep in mind, though, that fast-twitch fibers have little endurance. When contracting continually, they can only sustain five to ten seconds of maximum effort, and some research indicates that fast-twitch fibers will fatigue in just six to eight seconds. A minimum of thirty seconds rest is required for these fibers to recover. After successive efforts, you need even more rest, otherwise your slow-twitch fibers are called into play, and this is not what you want for a single, competitive lift. To emphasize, we are concerned with overloading and training fast-twitch muscle fibers, not slow-twitch. I suggest rest periods no longer than four minutes, because after that, the body cools off.

There are two phases, Preparation and Contest. I suggest Cluster Training during the last two weeks of Preparation and the first two weeks of Contest phases. The difference between the two is their intensity; the Contest phase demands less work and allows more rest. It might be shown in this way:

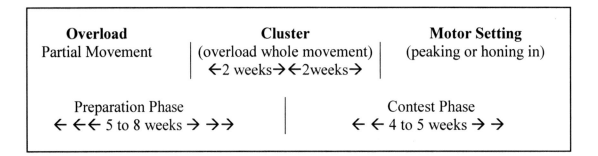

Chart 15 shows how this works. It outlines intensity, number of singles in a cluster, number of clusters and rest periods between singles in a cluster, and rest periods between clusters.

Cluster training can fit into other programs outlined in this book. I have listed three, four and five day programs in Chart 16 to demonstrate how it can be done. Workouts can take 1.5 to 2 hours. You might be worried about doing these clusters of singles, but remember that the percentages are within realistic capabilities, and adequate rest is built into the program. When completed, you will feel a refreshing overall fatigue, not the deadness that sometimes accompanies repetitions of partial movements or singles at higher intensities.

Movement	%	Singles	Clusters	Rest
Preparation Phase				
(first two weeks)				
Snatch	80-85	5-7	3-5	30-45 sec. between reps 1st 2 clusters
&				1.5 to 2 min. between 1st 2 clusters
Snatch Pulls (if	90-107	5-7	3-5	
pulls follow)				60 sec. between reps for next clusters
				2-3 min. between next clusters
Clean & Jerk	77-82	5-7	3-5	45-60 sec. between reps 1st 2 clusters
&				2-2.5 sec. between 1st 2 clusters
Clean Pulls (if pulls	90-107	5-7	3-5	
follow)				1-1.5 min. between reps next clusters
				3-3.5 min. between next clusters
Jerk Style	80-87	5-7	3-5	same as Snatch
Heavy Partial	95-115	5-7	3-5	30 sec. between reps 1st 2 clusters
Jerk Movemts				1.5 min. between
&				
Pulls (if pulls 1st in	95-112	5-7	3-5	45 sec. between reps next clusters
program)				2 min. between next clusters
Dead Lifts	100-117	5-7	3-5	30 sec. between reps 1st 2 clusters
(Olympic style)				1.5 min. between 1st 2 clusters
Squats	82-92	5-7	3-5	Same as Heavy Partial Jerk Movemts

Movement	%	Singles	Clusters	Rest
Contest Phase				
(second two weeks)				
Snatch	85-95	2-3	3-4	45-60 sec. between reps 1st 2 clusters
&				2 to 2.5 min. between 1st 2 clusters
Snatch Pulls (if	90-102	2-3	3-4	
pulls follow)				1-1.25 min. betwn reps next clusters
				3-3.5 min. between next clusters
Clean & Jerk	82-92	2-3	3-4	1-1.25 min. betwn reps next clusters
&				2.5-3 min. between 1st 2 clusters
Clean Pulls (if pulls	90-100	2-3	3-4	
follow)				1.5 min. between reps next cluster
				3.5-4 min. between next clusters
Jerk Style	85-85	2-3	3-4	same as Snatch
Heavy Partial	95-105	2-3	3-4	45 sec. between reps 1st 2 clusters
Jerk Movemts				2 min. between 1st 2 clusters
&				
Pulls (if pulls 1st in	92-105	2-3	3-4	1 min. between reps of next cluster
program)				3 min. between next clusters
Dead Lifts	95-105	2-3	3-4	45 sec. between reps 1st 2 clusters
(Olympic style)				2.5 min. between 1st 2 clusters
Squats	87-95	2-3	3-4	Same as Heavy Partial Jerk Movemts

Chart 15. Cluster Training

	3 Days per Week				
#1	Snatch Snatch Pulls Snatch Dead Lifts Legs	#2	Clean & Jerk Clean Pulls Clean Dead Lifts Legs	#3	Snatch Clean & Jerk Heavy Jerk Partial Movement Legs
	4 Days per Week				
#1	Snatch Snatch Pulls Snatch Dead Lifts Legs	#2	Clean & Jerk Clean Pulls Clean Dead Lifts Legs	#3	Snatch Clean & Jerk Snatch Pulls Clean Pulls
#4	Jerk from the Rack Heavy Jerk Partial Movement Snatch Dead Lifts Clean Dead Lifts Legs				
	5 Days per Week				
#1	Snatch Snatch Pulls Snatch Dead Lifts Legs	#2	Clean & Jerk Clean Pulls Clean Dead Lifts Legs	#3	Snatch Clean & Jerk Snatch Pulls Clean Pulls
#4	Jerk Style Heavy Jerk Partial Movement Legs			#5	Snatch Pulls Clean Pulls Snatch Dead Lifts Clean Dead Lifts

Chart 16. Example Cluster Training Schedule of Exercises

Remember Peary and Mabel's *Iron Man Magazine*, which recommended that lifters do maximum or near maximum presses from racks every minute for an hour? They reported excellent results.

12

Learning for Competition— Meeting Subgoals

I f motivational psychologists agree on anything, it's that goal setting is an important source of self motivation. E.A. Locke's theory of goal setting may be the closest thing there is to a law of nature in the behavioral sciences. According to Locke's theory, published in 1966, specific goals lead to a higher level of motivation and performance than having a generalized goal of "do your best," or having no goals at all.

That's why I've long made it a practice to write down my goals before each training session. It takes only a few minutes with my training diary. During or after every training session I write down my goals for next time. During weight workouts, I note whether I should repeat a movement, add weight or reps, change the exercise, whatever. After aerobic sessions, I record the workout and jot down ideas on what I should do next.

Try to make every training session a rewarding experience. Plan your workouts so they produce a feeling of accomplishment. If your workouts are filled with failure, you'll eventually get disgusted and quit. On the other hand, if you continually achieve specific results, you reinforce the training habit. Set yourself up for success. Set reasonable goals; that's very important.

—Clarence Bass, Former nationally ranked Olympic weightlifter, two-time Past-40 Mr. America, twice judged most muscular, author of nine books on weight training and health, former contributor to *Muscle and Fitness* magazine.

A successful meet involves more than being stronger than your competition. Psychology plays a big role in an athlete's performance. After months of hard training, there is a lot at stake when the lifter steps onto the platform. Many factors play into a successful, or failed, meet. The subtle and complex psychology of this sport is one of them.

Understanding the Stress of Competition

Play your own ballgame.
—Dick Green, top American Weightlifting Coach

When planning your periodized training program, it is important to establish goals. Your long-range goal is to post your best possible total in the important meets. This is the big goal that will shape the course of your training for a year or more. To remain motivated and challenged in the interim, it may be helpful to establish sub-goals. By meeting sub-goals successfully, you learn new tools and gain more confidence in lifting heavier weights under the pressure of the big meets.

Because we have so few competitors in the US, there are relatively few high level competitive meets in a given year. It can be difficult to accumulate experience and develop the confidence that ensures success. Every meet you attend will prepare you for the next.

That said, even very experienced lifters are affected by the pressure of competition. Take this into account and avert a pattern of failure and frustration. Here are some of the stressors you may encounter.

Consider that you may have to travel to a meet, and sometimes you'll go long distances to a competition. Once there, the surroundings often are unfamiliar. How often have you stayed at a hotel where your room is noisy or the bed is bad? The food is different, and the venue may feel strange when you venture far afield. Maybe you have a daunting opponent, or another competitor who intentionally intimidates.

Lifting is an individual sport; one contender lifts at a time, and all eyes are on that person on the platform. If competition makes you nervous, if you are not accustomed to being watched while you lift, regardless of your preparation, you may find it unsettling to lift in front of an audience.

Even a new platform can make a difference. In training, you lift on only one platform, and you become accustomed to it. In competition, you are confronted with two platforms. The warm up platform is different from the contest platform. Sometimes it is radically different, but radical or not, it is different, and some lifters are upset by this.

You often will contend with temperature and humidity changes. These can be general climate differences between your home and the location of the match, or it may be the difference between the warm up room and the contest area.

Some lifters don't learn to cope with microclimatic factors because they have not consciously recognized that they are issues.

The visual surroundings, such as the ambience of the platform space and the height of the ceiling, may require major adjustment. Don't expect every location to look the same, and learn to embrace variability. In 1957, the Senior National Weightlifting Championships was held in Daytona Beach, Florida. The outdoor venue disoriented so many lifters that more lifts were missed at that national meet than ever before.

You should anticipate using as many as three different makes of bars on the day of the meet: training, warm up and contest bars. They can be very different. When you are conscious of your response to this potential stressor, you can learn to cope with the stress if it arises.

Another adjustment you'll make, going from training to the structured framework of competition, is that in training you can take any weight at any time. In a contest, you lift when it is your turn, and your turn may not come according to your desires.

During training, your body weight should exceed your weight class limit by no more than 3.5 percent. In the next chapter I will discuss how to lose weight 24 hours before a meet. For now, let me say that doing so can be a big stressor.

If you train with straps, expect to total lower without them. Remember that you've given yourself an advantage during training, and don't stress about the difference between your training and contest lifts.

And finally, acknowledge that a contest means more to you than your regular training. It is one thing to lift against Joe Blow in a local contest, and it's another to lift in a large city, state, national or international competition against Joe Superman. The pressure increases considerably at each level. As one coach put it, "If you can't succeed in your local meet, how are you going to stand the pressure of world championships? Get in the habit of making only two or three lifts at a home meet, and you are going to bomb out, or have to start really light just to total." When you acknowledge the stress accompanying a big meet, it allows you to examine your own psychology and create sub-goals to address situations that might unnerve you. Focus on yourself and concentrate on what you are doing and ignore the competition.

As I have said before, competition is an important training tool. Your lifting will improve with every meet you enter, so enter as many as possible. Use each contest as an opportunity to learn more about yourself as a lifter and as a competitor. If you participate in a meet for which you have not peaked, use it as practice. Create challenges for yourself within the framework of every meet, and each experience will prepare you for the next.

While planning for my Olympic-style weightlifting camps, I developed a list of over 100 sub-goals to challenge and enliven a training program and prepare the athletes for competition. Part of that list is reproduced here, and I hope it will trigger more ideas from you.

- Use different warm ups. These can include physical or mental rehearsal. Start your lifts at a slow speed then build to faster speed. Use more complete movements or perform more singles. Try a brief warm up. Mix it up and experiment.
- Learn to use strategy. During the meet, choose a higher starting weight, and take small jumps in weight, especially in the snatch. Or choose a low starting weight, and try big or different jumps between attempts. Try to "build a total" in tight competition to force your rivals to take higher attempts than they prefer. This will pressure your opponents.
- Make last second changes and see how you react. Try waiting a little longer to step onto the platform after your name is called. Learn to compete by pressuring other lifters. Many don't know how to handle this situation and if you jump, it changes things for the opponents.
- Make body weight in a different way. See how you respond.
- Go to different lifting venues, get used to lifting in different settings.
- Attend meets where you lift at different times of day.
- Use a different Contest Peaking. Try it out and see how you react to it.
- Vary your day-of-meet routine and see how you react.
- Vary your clean and jerk to see if you can "pull one out of the hat." You may need it in a big competition. This may also be used to feel out big weights.
- Lift with total abandon. Don't think. Let yourself react. You are not going to lift heavier weights, at that point, thinking about form.
- Start with your best lift, or close to it, and put pressure on yourself for a second attempt.
- Meet goals based on last year's totals at the respective time of year. This is a must!
- Be a showman. See if you can get the crowd with you, even backstage while warming up. With the support of the audience, you have a great psychological advantage. Smile at the audience. Lift smoothly and precisely. Develop your own style.
- If you train with straps, vary the days before a contest that you stop using straps on lifts **and** pulls.
- Lift on different equipment, and if possible, lift at least once on the equipment that will be used in your big meet.

- Purposely lift where there are strict judges because the judging becomes stricter at higher caliber meets.
- Can you miss with a warm up weight and know enough to correct it so that it doesn't disrupt your warm ups?
- Try resting backstage before each warm up and between attempts. It is critical to know what to do between attempts and how to rest.
- Change your supplements and note the reaction.
- Try rough toweling your thighs or rubbing a brush over them, or pinching or pulling the trapezius to stimulate your muscles. This is grounded in physiology. Try it at various times.
- Get used to different types of lifting atmospheres, from quiet to noisy. Know what you want around you, and know how to adapt if you cannot control the situation.
- Let the 30-second buzzer go off while you are on the platform. Try to blot it out of your mind. If you can't bring yourself to do this, wait to go onto the platform till the buzzer goes off. There is plenty of time.
- Know yourself. Know what motivates you. Why do you lift? Is it the need to win, the need for self-expression, the crowd, the trophy, or the drive for self improvement? When the big contests come, use this to psych yourself.

Challenge yourself to explore these sub-goals and learn about yourself and competition. Know how to handle the stresses and pressures of a meet. If you can anticipate stressors and develop tools for dealing with them, you stand a much better chance of lifting to your full potential. If you do not prepare yourself appropriately, you really haven't trained for competition; you have only trained for lifting in the gym.

Notes

13

The White Moment—The Competition

*A*t the peak of tremendous effort, while the blood is pounding in your head, all suddenly becomes quiet within you. Everything seems clearer and whiter than before, as if great spotlights had been turned on. At that moment, you have conviction that you contain all the power in the world, that you are capable of everything, that you have wings. There is no more precious moment than this. You will work very hard for years to taste it again…and there is intense emotion after labor and sweat…the salty pleasure of the white moment!

—Yury Vlasov, former USSR World and Olympic heavyweight champion

After all the exertion and energy you've poured into training, the day of the meet finally arrives, and there still is more to do. First, you must make weight. Second, you select your opening attempts, and third, you warm up. After that, your tasks are to calm your mind, get out of your own way, and allow your training to take over. I'm going to expand on some of the good choices you can make to ensure your success.

Making Weight

For some lifters, the biggest challenge of a meet can be making weight. Ideally, throughout your training, your weight is around 3.5 percent higher than the top weight of your weight class. This way, you carry maximum muscle into competition. If your weight is more than 3.5 percent over the class limit, you will lose muscle and strength with any quick weight loss before a meet. If your weight is less than 3.5 percent above your weight class limit, you do not have the maximum amount of muscle for your class.

You can make your weight class as long as you don't weigh more than 3.5 percent over your class limit, and you can lose this weight in the 24 hours before weigh in with no loss of strength. This weight loss does take effort, and it entails some discomfort. The objective is to lose weight through a careful and controlled method of induced dehydration. Like I said, it involves some discomfort, but you will preserve strength. Here are some tips for losing the last couple of pounds and preserving strength, too.

Twenty-four hours before weigh in, have an easily digestible protein that will pass through your body quickly. Try small quantities of egg, low-fat milk or yogurt or low-sodium beef, chicken or fish broth. Avoid salt! I have seen lifters eat this way eighteen and even twelve hours before weigh in and still make weight, but this is usually not the case.

Drink only water or an electrolyte drink. At eighteen hours before weigh in, drink 19 – 24 ounces, and do not eat anything. At twelve hours before weigh in, drink 12 – 18 ounces. Six hours before weigh in, drink 8 – 12 ounces, and take 1200 mg of calcium and 2500 mg of potassium. These electrolytes, which are important in nerve impulse conduction and muscle coordination, can be lost when dehydration takes place. When taken hours in advance of weigh in, they will be absorbed in time to provide benefit for competition.

Be aware that you may even need to forego fluids 6 – 12 hours before weigh in! Remember, I said if you are no more than 3.5 percent above your weight class, you can lose the extra weight but there will be discomfort! However, discipline and effort will allow you to preserve maximum muscle and strength. Dropping weight in this way is effective, but you want to be very prepared for the experience. It is not fun.

A sauna can also promote dehydration, but make sure you are accustomed to it. If you are not, the weakness you feel afterwards can psych you into thinking you have lost strength. Do not stay in too long—no longer than ten minutes per session—and no more than three times in twenty-four hours. Too much fluid loss in this accelerated manner results in heavy electrolyte loss.

If you don't have to make weight, consider carbohydrate loading, three to two days out. Carbohydrate loading has been demonstrated to increase an athlete's energy. However, some evidence suggests that if done on a month in and month out basis, carbohydrate loading can have a detrimental effect on the body's digestive system. A good rule of thumb is to do it no more than once every three to four months. If losing weight is an issue for you, beware of carbohydrate loading. It causes the body to retain water. By the way, you can lose up to 2 pounds prior to the meet spitting into a cup.

After Weigh In

After the weigh in, sip an electrolyte drink or plain, cool water. It will taste wonderful, especially if you take 5 to 7 Tums for calcium and 2500 mg of potassium with it! Tums are one of the most easily absorbed calcium supplements on the market. Taken with an easily absorbed potassium source, you can replenish these minerals quickly before lifting. The ability to metabolize these minerals varies by individual, so the benefit for any one person is unpredictable. I recommend it as insurance, though.

I vividly remember an East German doctor giving a super heavyweight lifter a shot of something before warm up for the clean and jerk. I was horrified! I thought it was adrenaline or something similar. I called over an official and, when questioned, the doctor said the shot was an intravenous fluid of calcium and potassium. Even though the super heavyweight did not have to make weight, he worried a lot and worrying leaches electrolytes. They found the only way to get enough calcium, quickly, into his system was through intravenous injection. The practice had been approved by the Internatioal Weightlifting Federation.

An important note: When drinking fluids before and during a competition or training, drink them cold. The stomach capillaries will shrink and throw blood into the muscles. When fluids are warm, the capillaries relax, and blood is drawn from the muscles to the stomach, robbing the muscles of oxygen.

Between the weigh in and warm up, consume only liquids and some electrolytes. This is very important. Anything else is wasted and potentially harmful to your performance. Digestion takes blood from the muscles and could cause stomach upset. Lift hungry!

Before you warm up for the snatch, and during the snatch competition, you want to derive energy from a balanced source. You do not want sugar or simple carbohydrates that will cause your blood sugar levels to spike, followed later by a letdown.

In their book, *Nutrient Timing*, John Ivy and Robert Portman recommend using a drink (not solid food) with a ratio of 3-4 carbohydrates to 1 protein. I agree with this. It can be done in several ways, but always use a liquid. (A sport drink called *Accelerade* has been developed for this exact ratio. I am not working for this company and offer this only as information.) I would also use this drink cold right before, and during warm up, for the clean and jerk for a balanced pick-me-up.

Do not use caffeine until just before your warm up for the clean and jerk. Lifters are usually so psyched, and have so much energy for the snatch, that the caffeine is wasted. It can energize you too much and throw off your coordination. Save the caffeine for the clean and jerk warm up.

Selecting Contest Poundages

As I have discussed before, there are countless pressures associated with competition, and many variables can affect a lifter's performance. A new venue, different lighting, and a change in start times are a few things that may throw off a lifter and potentially sap confidence. This is very real, even to world class lifters, all of whom have become champions because they have learned to cope with stress.

Stress can be subtle, and you may not be conscious of its effect. It can play an important role in your performance and potentially undermine all your preparation. It is critical to recognize that stress is magnified when you choose starting weights that are too high.

Always select a starting weight that will lead to success. This sounds like an easy task; however, many lifters start too high. They fail to observe important cues about their frame of mind and readiness to attempt a specific weight.

In conversations with very experienced coaches, I have learned that few athletes can make their best lift on the second attempt. Because of that, choose a starting weight well below your personal best so that your first and second lifts will be successful. Success creates confidence and provides the basis for the intense concentration you'll need for your third attempt.

I remember working with a lifter who was determined to break his record in the snatch. We were touring and attending meets in different cities. He insisted on setting his first attempts very high. During the first meets of the tour, and after three countries, he completed only three attempts in the snatch. He made one successful attempt at each meet, yet his clean and jerk went well, and he established a personal best. At the next meet, after a long and persuasive talk, he asked for a lower first attempt. He came alive! After easily nailing his first attempt, he took big jumps on his second and third. He finally established the personal best he wanted.

Be flexible about your starting poundage. In training, vary your start weights and take different jumps in weight. When you are comfortable with this, your mind is more flexible about the weights you attempt and about big or little jumps; you are ready because you practice this in training. Don't get locked in on preplanned starting poundages when the situation is completely different than what you hoped for.

Pay attention to how you perform backstage because you'll gain valuable insights for choosing your starting poundage. Are you able to control the tempo of your warm up? You should start by lifting low weights slowly, and build up the speed of your lifts as the weight increases. Controlling the tempo of your lifts suggests that you are in command of your emotions.

Note your coordination as the warm ups proceed. Check your legs for chalk marks. If the bar is clean of chalk, rub some on it. How much of a chalk mark is on your thighs from the bar coming in contact with them? If the mark is heavy during warm up, your coordination is off; the bar is being pulled too far inward or is jerky. If you have no chalk mark, you are losing leverage. You want a brush with the bar that leaves a light mark. But brush or not, notice what the mark looks like in comparison to when you were "on" at some previous time.

Have someone watch your warm up lifts. Are your shoulders in front of the bar as you raise it to knee height? Is your back at the same angle in the start position as it is when the bar is at the knees? This is an indication of coordination and power in the big muscles of the legs, hips and back. Are your elbows out to the sides in the snatch? This is one of the first coordinated movements to go when a lifter is not "on." With elbows to the sides, you get good scapula rise. With elbows pointed back, the scapula will not rise as far, and more swing will take place at the top.

Visualize what you are to do. Have another lifter, or coach, demonstrate the motion for you slowly. This will make more sense to you than words. Any words should be simple and meaningful. Don't clutter your mind with a lot of thought. You want a few cues that will allow things to happen automatically.

Some lifters respond to key phrases. Know what works and use only a few simple ones. In the heat of competition, only basic, familiar prompts are meaningful. The rest goes in one ear and out the other. Some examples are: push with the legs, enter in, keep the back at an angle, wait for the pop, reach, extend, finish. Convert the key words and the visualization into the "feeling" you want to experience with the lift. It is simple. It is internalized, and it is the best formula for the best results.

Another backstage guideline for choosing starting poundages is to keep in mind where you are in a training cycle. Early in the season, you have done more multiple repetitions at lower weights and fewer singles at higher weights. Late in the season, you have practiced more singles, for a longer period of time. After this, you can expect more of a weight difference between the second and third attempts.

Another clue that will help you determine the weight of your first attempt is how well you engage people backstage. This is a minor audience. Some lifters capture the attention of other lifters because of the quality of their lifts. This boosts a lifter's confidence. Audience support can make a big difference in your performance. If you lift smoothly backstage and are inspired by the reaction of others, this probably indicates higher starting poundage. Similarly, good audience reaction when you are on stage may indicate bigger jumps in poundage on succeeding attempts. Poor audience reaction to your lifts may indicate smaller jumps. I emphasize this audience response. Win over the audience. It will help you.

Still another backstage guideline is your ability to concentrate. The greater your concentration, the more nerve fibers are activated, hence, more muscle fibers are activated. Allow me to paraphrase the great American lifting coach, Dick Smith, and his description of concentration, "When a photographer takes a picture of a bee on a flower in a field of flowers he tries to blur out everything but that one bee and that one flower." I think Smith describes well the intense concentration required to lift heavy weights. Be honest with yourself. Let's face it, not every lifter can be "up" for every meet. If you cannot concentrate, admit it to yourself. Start lower and get something positive out of the meet. Who knows, as you experience some success, you might even get into the swing of things. If you begin with a high starting weight when you cannot concentrate, however, is to invite disaster.

Anybody can do poorly in their warm ups. Despite how prepared you are, occasionally, no matter what you do, you are going to struggle. This will be one of those contests where you should lower your expectations, and take as much success out of the competition as possible. Be happy for small rewards. If you ignore the subtle warning signs in your warm ups, you're asking for negative and destructive results.

Athletes need to progress slowly and build on success. A bad experience during competition may hinder your progress unless you're able to derive value from it. An extreme example of this is boxing. Overmatched and really beaten, a boxer never recovers psychologically. I want you to lift well and progress as fast as possible. Sometimes that means making the most of a bad situation. This is better than nothing.

Selecting Contest Warm Ups

There are many different ways to warm up. Find one that suits you.

Stretch for 15 to 20 minutes before you warm up. Manual stretching is preferred, with warm water applied to the ankle and wrist joints, which are difficult joints to warm. Begin your warm up lifts at about 50 percent of your starting attempt, although it is wise to use an even lower percentage if your confidence is shaky. At most, do two repetitions with light weights, under 40 percent of your maximum. Then practice singles with heavier weights.

The last warm up should be completed about 3-5 minutes before your first attempt. In a contest where there is a long wait, do a lift with 80 to 85 percent every three to five minutes. The lift doesn't have to be complete—lift the weight but do not come up with it—dump it. Five or six sets of warm ups are good for the snatch. Four or five sets are sufficient for the clean and jerk. You should rest for 3 to 4 minutes between sets.

Keep moving. Do not sit for more than 3 1/2 minutes. Get up and move around so your joints are free for blood circulation when you are sitting. Sit with your legs somewhat propped up, if possible, or extended in front, with a slight bend in the knee.

Massage with firm circular motions between attempts is helpful. Try to include tendon attachments with smaller motions, and do not push muscle and tendon over bone. End the massage by firmly and gently slapping the area.

Robert Ansovitch Roman, a highly respected coach in the former USSR, developed a precise warm up system. Roman was a master at taking the science of exercise physiology and biomechanics and applying it to Olympic-style weightlifting, training and competition. During our tour of Europe in 1974, our young lifters were impressed by the warm up methods employed by the Europeans. Our lifters were accustomed to practicing many repetitions, lots of them from the thigh, and going fast. They were literally wearing themselves out, wasting time, and not practicing their warm ups in the motions of the competition: one full repetition from the floor on the competitive platform.

The following summarizes Roman's warm up method:

- Increase the height of the pull 3 inches from the 1st to the 3rd practice lifts.
- From the 4th through the 6th practice lifts, the height of the pull remains the same.
- The best technique occurs between the 3rd and 5th and does not deteriorate until the 10th.
- He recommends two high pulls with the weight you plan for your first attempt.
- If the wait is longer than 3 to 5 minutes, do a high pull with your next attempt.

Here is what it is like in practice:

- Stretch for 15 minutes and practice some light overhead squats and split squats.
- Practice your single lift, slowly, for five to seven minutes and feel the leverage positions. Use roughly 60 percent wof your starting attempt.

Do either power or complete movements.

- Complete one snatch at each of the percentages listed below. Allow one and a half to two minutes rest between each lift:

  ◊   Snatch 100%   60, 70, 75, 80, 85, 90%   2 Pulls

  ◊   Clean & Jerk 100%   70, 75, 80, 85, 90%   2 Pulls

As you can see, no time is wasted. Let me stress that with lighter weight, you practice the lift as though in slow motion. You cannot practice proper coordination patterns with lighter weights during your warm up if you lift too fast. Incorporate Roman's warm up guidelines and you can lift with confidence when your name is called.

Remember that the warm up is intended to prepare you and your muscles for competition. Even if the wait between attempts runs long, you must stay warm. After about three minutes, the body starts to cool off. At the end of five minutes, it is really cooling off, and muscle temperature, contractibility and flexibility diminish.

If you have to wait more than five minutes between your attempts, after completing this warm up, take a lift or do a high pull using 80 to 85 percent of your next attempt. If you are warming up for the clean and jerk, clean the weight and then dump it. The idea is to keep warm and conserve energy, too. A pull requires less energy than a complete lift. It takes a lot of energy to stand up with the weight, which is the reason for dropping the weight after catching it.

Overcoming Nerves

Nerves can interfere with concentration. It is better not to think too much because your mind can get in the way of all the training your body has done. A little time thinking about what you are supposed to do is better than a lot of time worrying. The following methods have been used successfully to distract and focus a nervous lifter.

Ideally, a coach or friend will watch the lifting order and help you keep track of your turn. When you are about four attempts from your turn, a coach or training partner can manually stretch your knees, wrists, hips, groin and shoulders. This helps distract you from fear and anxiety. By the time you are on deck, you should be ready to concentrate. If you don't have control of your nerves, your coach may shake your shoulders hard, give your rear end or back a hard slap, or even lay a sharp clap on your face to help you focus. There are reticular fibers in the head, and a jolt brings them around pretty quickly.

I remember working with one lifter who, over and over again, was unable to concentrate and repeatedly missed his lifts. I told him that a sharp slap to both sides of his head would help him focus. When his name was called, I took him away from the audience so that we were out of their sight, stood right in front of him and slapped him hard. He looked shocked but lifted well.

This method should not be used on just any lifter, but there are some for whom no amount of confidence building seems to help. For this type of lifter, something sharp and jolting is often the only distraction from their fear. I am not saying you should try this, but in case you do, make sure no one is watching. They wouldn't understand!

Competition Strategy

After your first attempt of the contest on the platform, how do you determine the weight of your next lift? To answer that question, know your opponents. If you are competing against another athlete for a place in the top five or ten, know what they lift. Know their snatch, know their clean and jerk and know their totals. If you are in a good position in the competition, especially in the snatch, take a weight that is below your best. This takes pressure off you and helps you build your total. It might put pressure on the other guy to take his best, or over his best, on his second attempt.

Because the snatch is the first lift, be conservative. The success of your meet may be riding on it. Be successful in your first two attempts because they lay the groundwork for attempting a maximum effort with your third. So many complications can arise that I have one more guideline to offer. Sneak up on the snatch; do not take wild jumps. With the third attempt, even one additional kilo on the bar looks awfully good going into the clean and jerk. Once you have established success in the snatch, you can be more aggressive with the clean and jerk. If you want to jump big, do it after the first clean and jerk. By then you have established a good total in the snatch, and you have added a successful first clean and jerk. Now it is a contest! With three or four successes under your belt at this stage, you should be set to pour it on.

I hope I have made it clear that you need to alleviate the pressure of competition to make any progress. Do not start high on your first attempt. You create too much pressure when you do, and it robs you of your concentration, which can severely interfere with your lifting.

If you adopt the guidelines I have suggested, you will have a solid baseline from which to select your contest poundages. Everything is designed to help you realize your potential. It is really wonderful to see a lifter, who has learned the correct lifting techniques and has put together a good training plan, come to a meet, select poundage wisely and make at least five attempts. It is even better when a lifter sets personal records and attains the highest rank possible. The rules give a lifter six attempts, not two, so make optimal use of them.

Recovering From Workouts and Competition

In all likelihood, you will be extremely tired after the competition. You have been training relentlessly for months, lifted weights as heavy as you could tolerate, and afterwards, your body, emotions and spirit will be exhausted. Here are a few methods for assisting your recovery.

As much as possible, remove the waste products built up during training and competition. Your muscles will recover faster and you'll reduce the chance of injury. Begin with a two or three minute hot shower to draw the intercellular fluid from the capillaries and into the cells. Increasing fluid in the cells dilutes the toxins. Next, turn the shower to cool or cold (the cooler the better) for 15 seconds. The cells constrict and squeeze the excess fluid and toxins into the intercellular space, where they enter the circulatory system and are carried off. Alternate hot and cold showers four or five times for best results, ending with the cool or cold shower.

You can also remove waste products from the cells by alternating a steam bath or sauna with a swim in a pool or a dip in the snow. If you have never tried this form of recovery, you are in for a pleasant surprise. You will have little or no soreness and a really fresh feeling. If you take a hot shower, steam bath or sauna and do not follow it with cool or cold water allows excess fluid into the cells. Because of the excess fluid, the cells stretch and impinge on nerve fibers. This increases the chance of a muscle cell rupture. At the same time, the cell is still wallowing in its own filth and recovery is slowed.

Lifters should also consider checking their blood pressure on the morning after a meet. If you have a cuff, take your blood pressure upon waking. If this waking blood pressure is 15 percent higher than your waking blood pressure of the previous day, reduce the training for the day. When the waking blood pressure returns to normal, continue your regular workout. Lactic acid in your blood may cause an elevation of blood pressure.

Here is another tip from John Ivy and Robert Portman's book, *Nutrient Timing*. They recommend a carbohydrate to protein level of 4 to 1 within 45 minutes of completing a meet or work out to aid recovery. I highly agree with this. There is a product called Endurox R4 with the ratio of 3-4 to 1. This aids recovery by providing the correct balance of protein to carbohydrates to repair and build muscle.

14

Weight for Flexibility

lexibility is largely determined by genetics. This means there are natural limitations to our flexibility, yet most everyone can improve at least a little. And in Olympic lifting, a little can mean a lot. In this chapter, I will discuss various methods of stretching and why you must do it, but not over do it.

We are born with a certain balance of elastic and collagenous muscle fibers. Both are needed. Collagenous fibers stabilize the joints. Elastic fibers allow our joints mobility and permit quickness.

For the sport of Olympic weightlifting, this balance of muscle fibers permits the body segments to move into the correct position at the right time. Healthy flexibility allows joints to find the best mechanical leverage and stability. I have seen studies in tennis, discus, shot and javelin that show for every one-quarter inch of flexibility gained, capacity for power dramatically improves. This is clearly true for lifters.

If you want to be flexible in the range of motion required by your sport, then you must stretch in the positions typical of your sport. In athletic training, this is called mimicry. Mimicry is important, whether you are trying to develop flexibility or strength.

Mimicry is desired because the more closely an exercise or stretch resembles the sport for which you are training, the more valuable that exercise or stretch will be. For example, in weightlifting, we want to mimic the movements of the lifts as we train for flexibility. We practice for mobility and increased athletic leverage, which is a function of flexibility. This is called transfer. For meaningful transfer to take place, you must get specific.

Some athletic movements cannot be precisely duplicated. This is especially true of dynamic athletic motion. Even if the movement can be duplicated, training for flexibility in the motion, with sufficient intensity, can risk injury. Logic suggests that we take the motion apart and practice components, but there is a risk in this, too. A movement can be so isolated in training that it cannot be fit back into the complete movement. The coordination pattern gets out of sync. In the case of stretching, it is better to stretch a muscle in the desired coordination pattern.

Still, some static stretching is valuable. In my experience, holding a static stretch for 20 to 40 is very effective. By static, I mean that when you reach the end point of your flexibility, you hold that position for a period of time. You want a strong stretch, but not so strong that tearing takes place. Keep in mind that, like everything, you can get too much of a good thing. You can stretch too much, but I did not fully understand this until I saw the Chinese compete at the 1978 World Weightlifting Championships. The Chinese team did minimal stretching because too much static stretching "milks" the fluid from the cell, which diminishes muscle tension. Muscle tension is part of strength, and it is related, in part, to sufficient hydration of the muscle cells.

With a longer static stretch, like upwards of two minutes, you can gain extra flexibility. You are trading strength for flexibility, though, because after the long stretch you really are weaker. It is best to be cautious and not overdo the long stretches.

There are different ways to achieve a beneficial stretch. A tired muscle stretches more readily. An excellent way to capitalize on this is to contract the muscle for 5 seconds; then stretch it for 15. Do this with the joint straight and again with the joint slightly bent.

Try this. Slowly bend and straighten a joint, 5 times in 45 seconds to one minute. This moves the stretch from the muscle's point of origin to its insertion, or vice versa. This way, you're stretching the whole length of the muscle. This is a very effective stretching progression. (Notice that we always use a progression of intensity, even in stretching.)

You also can stretch manually. Your coach or training partner uses his or her own strength to push or pull you into a stretch position that you cannot achieve yourself.

Some of our stretches can be done in very warm water in a shower or bathtub, and in a warm swimming pool or hot tub. Physical therapists have done manual stretching in warm water for years.

Not all static stretches will increase flexibility. The opposite muscle group can inhibit the stretch and has to be overcome for the stretch to work. Ballistic stretching is one answer to this problem. Ballistic means the bone is moving so fast that it outruns the muscle. At the very end of the movement, the muscle catches up and tugs hard on the bone. You can do ballistic stretches safely and achieve excellent results.

Ballistic stretches went out of vogue because people were not warming up sufficiently beforehand. You must warm and stretch your muscles first to avoid injury during ballistic stretches. When your muscles are sufficiently warmed and stretched statically, the muscle is rendered pliable enough to accept a ballistic stretch. When you take this precaution, your results are outstanding.

I believe ballistic stretching is an excellent method of stretching. Some athletics incorporate ballistic movements, including Olympic lifting. For example, the split rebound to the bottom position of the jerk and snatch are ballistic motions. If you stretch in this way, which is called mimicry, you're stretching muscles the same way that is demanded of them in your sport.

Ten seconds is the best duration for most ballistic motions, which is practical for stretching the fast-twitch muscle fibers. As a reminder, flexibility of the fast-twitch muscle fibers is important in Olympic lifting. The contractile time of fast-twitch fibers is usually ten seconds, and they tire in 6 to 12 seconds.

Flexibility Progression—Non-Weighted Stretches

1) Stretch the muscle statically for 20 – 40 seconds
2) Contract the muscle 5 seconds and then stretch for 15 seconds
3) Contract the muscle 5 seconds and then stretch it for 15 seconds, with the joint straight and then bent. Each position gets 15 seconds.
4) Slowly bend and straighten the joint five times
5) Manually: stretch statically for 20 – 40 seconds
   Contract 5 seconds, stretch 15 seconds- two times

Flexibility Progression—Weighted Stretches

1) With dumbbells or barbell hold a static stretch 20 – 40 seconds
2) Push up or pull down to contract the muscle 5 seconds with weight. Then perform a static stretch position for 15 seconds. Do this two times.
3) Push up or pull down, as the case may be, for 5 seconds and stretch for 15 seconds with the joint straight and then bent
4) Slowly bend and straighten the joint five times so the stretch moves slowly along the muscle.

Flexibility Progression—Ballistic Stretches

The most effective way to stretch for the two Olympic lifts is to stretch in the same position as receiving the bar. It teaches consistent position, which is so necessary when lifting heavy weights. Ballistic stretching takes place when the lifter drops into the full squat position when catching the bar. The ankles and hips are subjected to the ballistic motion. I recommend practicing these stretches with a light bar or even a broomstick.

1) Ballistic Split Snatch—Hold the broomstick overhead with a snatch grip and drop rapidly into a split (or lunge) position (front foot flat and knee bent with the back leg extended, resting on the ball of the foot). Arms are straight and the elbows are locked out, by pushing up and outward against the broomstick.

2) Ballistic Squat Snatch—With the broomstick overhead, using a snatch grip, drop quickly into a squat with arms extended and elbows in locked out position.

3) Ballistic Split Jerk—Hold the bar overhead with a jerk grip. Drop rapidly into a split or lunge position, pushing up and out on the bar.

If you use the split style, remember, and this is important, the split of the jerk is not as deep as the split of the clean. When the hips drop too low, the arms tend to move backward to counter balance the position, and the upraised arms, hands and bar end up behind the lifter's head. If you develop the habit of dropping your hips, you risk injury as you lift heavier weights. Experience shows that even with great shoulder flexibility, shoulder stability is compromised with an overhead weight and jerk grip. The humerus cannot be supported sufficiently in the shoulder socket with this close grip.

There are a few lifting immortals who have gone as low in the jerk as in the clean, but they are rare. One is the great Olympic and World Champion Waldemar Baszanowski of Poland. While executing the jerk in his final lift at the 1964 Olympics, he tossed the bar slightly out front. He split down and forward, catching the bar behind his head with a jerk grip! I was there and heard an audible sigh from the Japanese team. (When the Japanese sigh, they are very impressed!)

I am an example of the norm. I was trying to break a US master record and got really low on the 341 pound jerk. I secured the lift, but my shoulders were black and blue for weeks from the tearing that resulted.

4) Ballistic Squat Jerk—What can I say? I mean, is it possible? It is, but for incredibly few lifters. Most notably, some Chinese lifters on the world scene have stable and flexible enough shoulders to do it successfully. It is a great style, but very few people have the shoulder stability or flexibility to do it without injury. See the Ballistic Squat Snatch, but with a jerk grip.

5) Ballistic Split Clean—Standing with the bar across the chest at shoulder level, drop into a split. See Split Snatch.

We use the following stretches in our programs at my gym. There are many more flexibility exercises. The methods presented here may inspire other flexibility exercises of your own.

Ankle Stretches

1) Ankle Stretch—Lean against something for stability, and assume a split or lunge position. Press the heel of the extended back leg toward the floor. Feel the stretch in your calf. Hold for 20 – 40 seconds.

2) Ankle Stretch—Using the same position as above, slowly bend the knee of the extended back leg. As you slightly bend the knee of the extended leg, your heel comes slightly off the floor. As you straighten the knee, your heel returns to the floor. Repeat 5 times each side. The stretch moves from the top of your calf, at the knee, to the bottom of the calf, above the ankle.

3) Ankle Stretch on Calf Machine—Stand with the ball of the foot on the platform and your heels extending off it. Raise your heels and remain on balls of feet for 5 seconds, then allow your heels to drop below the balls of your feet. Hold for 15 seconds. Repeat this twice.

4) Ankle Stretch on Prostretch—I am wary of gimmicks, but this inexpensive apparatus definitely works. Place your foot onto the Prostretch, with the heel fitted into the cup, and tilt your ankle back so you feel a strong stretch in your calf. Hold for 15 seconds.

Front Thigh Stretches

1) Split Squat—This stretches the front thigh when your leg is extended. Assume a split position, with the front knee bent at a right angle. Your knee is over the ankle. The other leg is extended behind you, with your knee slightly bent. Your back heel is off the floor. Think of pressing the hip of your extended leg forward. In this position, your front knee and back are protected. Hold for 20 – 40 seconds

2) Split Squat—Assume the split squat stance described above. Slowly bend and straighten the back knee. Repeat 5 times on each side.

3) Split with Weight—Assume the split stance, again. Holding dumb bells, or with a bar on the shoulders, make short up-and-down motions by slightly

lowering and then raising the hips. Do this for 5 seconds. Then lower into a deeper split position, and hold for 15 seconds. Repeat this twice.

4) Split Squat with Weight using #2 above—Hold the barbell overhead, like the snatch, or on the front shoulders, as in the squat clean. Repeat as in Stretch #2 above.

Back Thigh Stretches

1) Seated Back Thigh Stretch—Sit on the floor with your legs together and your knees slightly bent. Reach for your feet and hold. You may only be able to reach your ankles or calves. That's fine. Allow your back to arch and your knees to bend slightly. If your flexibility is limited, place a rope around the soles of your feet, and hold the rope in each hand on either side of your legs to help you stretch.

2) Back Thigh Stretch with Rope on Ball of Foot—Recline on the floor or a mat. Place one foot flat on the floor with your knee bent. Place a rope around the toe of the other foot, and extend that leg toward the ceiling. Slowly bend the knee of the extended leg, bringing your knee downward, toward your shoulder, until you feel a strong stretch in back of your thigh near your buttock. Then straighten slowly. Repeat 5 times for each leg. You will feel the stretch move from a point on the hamstring near your knee to the buttock.

3) Split with Weight—With dumb bells in hands, or bar on shoulders, assume the split stance. Make short up-and-down motions by bending and straightening the knees. (Note that the knees never lock out; they remain slightly bent even in extension.) Do this for five seconds. Then lower into a deeper split position and hold for 15 seconds. Repeat this twice.

4) Squat with Weight #3—Hold a barbell overhead, like the snatch, or on your front shoulders, as in the squat clean. Repeat as in Stretch #3 above.

Inner Thigh Stretches

1) Seated Inner Thigh Stretch—You will need a stretching bar mounted on a wall. Sit on the mat, facing the wall just in front of the bar. Spread your legs wide, and place your feet against the wall beneath the bar. Reach for a bar and pull your chest into the bar. The position is most effective if you sit with your chest lifted and back straight. Pull as close as you need to get a good stretch.

2) Seated One Leg Inner Thigh Stretch—Sit on a mat, legs spread as wide as is comfortable. Bring one foot into the groin so that the side thigh and calf of the bent leg are resting on the floor. Try to keep both buttocks in contact with the floor as you lean forward, over the extended leg.

3) Half Lotus—This stretch is borrowed from Yoga. Sit on the floor with one foot pulled into the groin, knee tightly bent and side of leg resting on the floor. Take the opposite foot and place it on top of the knee, or even thigh, of the bent leg. If necessary to feel a deeper stretch, press downward gently on the knee of the crossing leg.

4) Wide Stance Squat—This standing stretch is called a plie in a ballet studio. It can be done with or without weight. Assume a wide stance, feet turned slightly outward. Your chest is lifted. Maintain a curve in your lower back. Your knees are aligned over your ankles and in line with the position of your toes.

Low Back Stretches

1) Seated Lower Back Stretch—Sit on the floor, with your knees bent and the soles of your feet together. You knees will fall open toward the floor. Lean forward with your torso to achieve the desired stretch. Allow your back to round, and if you desire more of a stretch, open your knees slightly.

2) Plough with Knees Bent and Wide—Seated on a comfortable surface, roll onto your back, and throw your feet over your head until your toes are touching, or almost touching, the floor behind your head. Allow your knees to drop alongside, or in back of, your head. It is very important that your knees are bent and wide, thus stretching more of your lower back and iliosacral joint than your back thigh.

3) Hang from Support with Feet against Wall—Approach a stretching bar that is at roughly chest height. Grip the bar with both hands, have your feet shoulder width apart, and place your toes against the wall. Allow your hips to drop and knees to bend slightly. Your back will round gently. Hold for 15 seconds.

4) Rounded Back Weighted Stretch—Stand with your feet at shoulder width. Round your back and roll forward so that you feel a stretch. You can do this stretch with dumb bells or a barbell, and if you require more of a stretch, stand on a box or step. Keep your knees slightly bent in this stretch. This stretch promotes stability in your back and removes the strong stretch from your hamstring. Use caution when coming up. It is a good idea to leave the weights on the floor before returning to an upright, standing position.

Hip Stretches

1) Split Squat—With dumb bells in your hands or the bar on your shoulders, assume the split stance. Make short up-and-down motions by slightly lowering and then raising the hips. Think of pressing the hip of your back extending leg, forward. Do this for 5 seconds. Then lower into a deeper split position and hold for 15 seconds. Repeat this twice.

2) Split Squat-Slowly Bend and Straighten Knee—With the barbell held overhead, like the snatch, or on your front shoulders, repeat as in Stretch #1 above.

3) Wide Stance Squat—Same as #4 Inner Thigh Stretches

4) Half Lotus—This stretch is borrowed from Yoga. Sit on the floor with one foot pulled into the groin, knee tightly bent and leg resting on the floor. Take the opposite foot and place it on top of the thigh of the bent leg. If necessary to feel a deeper stretch, press downward gently on the knee of the crossing leg.

5) Lying Hip Stretch—You will need a stretching bar for this exercise. Lie face down on the floor, head close to the wall and body perpendicular to it. Loop a rope around your ankle and over a low bar. Use the rope to raise your leg from the hip joint and from the floor. By pulling down on the rope, you will pull your lower leg back, in the direction of the wall. Bend your knees slightly to take the strain off your back.

Shoulder—External Rotation Stretches

1) Corner Stretch—Stand, facing a corner. Step forward with one foot, placing it into the corner; this extends your back leg behind you, similar to a split or lunge. With your elbows bent at right angles and your upper arms parallel to the floor, place your forearms against the two walls. Press your chest forward and into the corner, while the forearms remain in a fixed position on the adjacent walls. Stand close to the corner, but far enough away to be able to lean into the position.

2) Hand Behind Head—Find a corner or doorframe. With one hand placed on the back of your head, rest the elbow of that arm on an open doorframe and assume a split or lunge position. The upper arm should be parallel to the floor. Press forward with your chest, to feel a stretch through the front of your shoulder and side chest. For more stretch, turn your torso slightly away from the raised arm.

3) Both Hands Behind Head—I consider this one of our best stretches, but it does require a partner. Place both hands behind your head, and allow your partner to gently pull your elbows back and toward each other.

4) Bar Hang—Hang from a bar or rings with palms externally rotated.

Shoulder—Internal Rotation Stretches

1) Support Stretch on Bar—Stand with your back to a bar that is just above waist height. Grip the bar behind you with a wide, snatch grip. The upper arms remain parallel to the floor and elbows are bent at right angles. The elbows are also lifted so that the upper arms and chest form a straight line. The elbows do not drop in back of you. Sink downward with the hips into the stretch position.

2) Manual One Arm Internal Rotation—This stretch requires the assistance of a partner. Stand with your arms at your sides, chest lifted. Stretch your right shoulder by bending your elbow until the forearm is perpendicular to the floor and behind your back, which will be at or near waist level. Your partner should stand behind you to stabilize your shoulder as he lifts the right arm gently upward. Repeat for the left shoulder.

3) Manual Two Arm Internal Rotation—This is another partner stretch. Stand with your arms straight at your sides, with your stretching partner behind you. Rotate your arms at the shoulder so that your palms are facing forward or even slightly toward the back. Bending at the waist removes the stretch from your shoulders, so you must remain upright for this stretch to be effective. With your partner behind you, raise your arms upwards as he or she gently moves them inwards and toward each other.

4) Hang on Bent Bar—With your hands on an angle bar or free rings, with the palms turned outward, an internal rotation is achieved.

Shoulder Flexion

1) Kneeling Shoulder/Chest Stretch—In Yoga, this stretch is called the Downward Facing Dog. Kneel on the floor, with your hips on your calves. Reach forward and place your palms and forearms on the floor. Your hips will come off your calves at this point. Slide your hands forward as you bring your chest to the floor. This will raise your hips toward the ceiling, and your shins will remain in contact with the floor. You will have a deep curve in your spine when you do this correctly, and you will feel a strong stretch in your shoulders and chest.

2) Rope Shoulder/Chest Stretch—Hold a rope in one hand, raise that arm to point your elbow to the ceiling, and let the rope drop down your back. Take the rope with your free hand and gently pull down on it.

3) Pulley Shoulder/Chest Stretch—Same as #2 but done on a pulley.

4) Jerk Split Squat with Bar—With a light weight or broomstick overhead, push up on the bar so your elbows remain straight, and split squat as low as possible, keeping the bar overhead. If the bar goes in front of your head, the squat is too low for the amount of flexibility. If the bar goes in back of your head, and you cannot squat lower, you need a closer grip.

The Miller Fitness Plan, Physical Training for Men and Women, 2005. Sunstone Press, Santa Fe, New Mexico.

Olympic Training Manual, 1977. Ironman Industries, Alliance, Nebraska.

Weight Training for your Specific Sport, 1976. Ironman Industries, Alliance, Nebraska.

How to Teach Weightlifting in High School & College, 1968. Shimizu Printing, Kobe, Japan.

CPSIA information can be obtained at www.ICGtesting.com
Printed in the USA
LVOW090717191212

312355LV00001B/9/P

9 780865 348110